EDGAR ALLAN POE

THE CHELSEA HOUSE LIBRARY OF BIOGRAPHY

EDGAR ALLAN POE

SUZANNE LeVERT

Chelsea House Publishers

New York • Philadelphia

CHELSEA HOUSE PUBLISHERS

Editor-in-Chief Richard S. Papale
Managing Editor Karyn Gullen Browne
Copy Chief Philip Koslow
Picture Editor Adrian Allen
Art Director Maria Epes
Assistant Art Director Howard Brotman
Manufacturing Director Gerald Levine
Systems Manager Lindsey Ottman
Production Manager Joseph Romano
Production Coordinator Marie Claire Cebrián

The Chelsea House Library of Biography
Senior Editor Kathy Kuhtz

*Staff for **EDGAR ALLAN POE***
Copy Editor Christopher Duffy
Editorial Assistant Michele Berezansky
Picture Researcher Sandy Jones
Series Designer Basia Niemczyc
Cover Illustration Maria Josenhans

Printed and bound in Mexico.

First Printing

1 3 5 7 9 8 6 4 2

Library of Congress Cataloging-in-Publication Data

LeVert, Suzanne.
Edgar Allan Poe/by Suzanne LeVert.
p. cm.—(The Chelsea House library of biography)
Includes bibliographical references and index.
Summary: A biography of the imaginative, tempestuous author and poet, focus-
ing on his struggles to establish himself in the literary world.
ISBN 0-7910-1640-4
      0-7910-1644-7 (pbk.)
1. Poe, Edgar Allan, 1809–49—Biography—Juvenile literature. 2. Authors,
American—19th century—Biography—Juvenile literature. [1. Poe, Edgar
Allan, 1809–49. 2. Authors, American.] I. Title. II. Series.
PS2631.L46 1992   91-39113
818'.309—dc20   CIP
[B]   AC

Contents

THE CHELSEA HOUSE LIBRARY OF BIOGRAPHY

Barbara Bush	Jack London
John C. Calhoun	Horace Mann
Clarence Darrow	Muhammad
Charles Darwin	Edward R. Murrow
Anne Frank	William Penn
William Lloyd Garrison	Edgar Allan Poe
Martha Graham	Norman Schwarzkopf
J. Edgar Hoover	Joseph Smith
Saddam Hussein	Sam Walton
Jesse James	Frank Lloyd Wright
Rose Kennedy	Boris Yeltsin
John Lennon	Brigham Young

Other titles in the series are forthcoming.

Introduction

Learning from Biographies

Vito Perrone

The oldest narratives that exist are biographical. Much of what we know, for example, about the Pharaohs of ancient Egypt, the builders of Babylon, the philosophers of Greece, the rulers of Rome, the many biblical and religious leaders who provide the base for contemporary spiritual beliefs, has come to us through biographies—the stories of their lives. Although an oral tradition was long the mainstay of historically important biographical accounts, the oral stories making up this tradition became by the 1st century A.D. central elements of a growing written literature.

In the 1st century A.D., biography assumed a more formal quality through the work of such writers as Plutarch, who left us more than 500 biographies of political and intellectual leaders of Rome and Greece. This tradition of focusing on great personages lasted well into the 20th century and is seen as an important means of understanding the history of various times and places. We learn much, for example, from Plutarch's writing about the collapse of the Greek city-states and about the struggles in Rome over the justice and the constitutionality of a world empire. We also gain considerable understanding of the definitions of morality and civic virtue and how various common men and women lived out their daily existence.

Not surprisingly, the earliest American writing, beginning in the 17th century, was heavily biographical. Those Europeans who came to America were dedicated to recording their experience, especially the struggles they faced in building what they determined to be a new culture. John Norton's *Life and Death of John Cotton*, printed in 1630, typifies these early works. Later biographers often tackled more ambitious projects. Cotton Mather's *Magnalia Christi Americana*, published in 1702, accounted for the lives of more than 70 ministers and political leaders. In addition, a biographical literature around the theme of Indian captivity had considerable popularity. Soon after the American Revolution and the organization of the United States of America, Americans were treated to a large outpouring of biographies about such figures as Benjamin Franklin, George Washington, Thomas Jefferson, and Aaron Burr, among others. These particular works served to build a strong sense of national identity.

Among the diverse forms of historical literature, biographies have been over many centuries the most popular. And in recent years interest in biography has grown even greater, as biography has gone beyond prominent government figures, military leaders, giants of business, industry, literature, and the arts. Today we are treated increasingly to biographies of more common people who have inspired others by their particular acts of courage, by their positions on important social and political issues, or by their dedicated lives as teachers, town physicians, mothers, and fathers. Through this broader biographical literature, much of which is featured in the CHELSEA HOUSE LIBRARY OF BIOGRAPHY, our historical understandings can be enriched greatly.

What makes biography so compelling? Most important, biography is a human story. In this regard, it makes of history something personal, a narrative with which we can make an intimate connection. Biographers typically ask us as readers to accompany them on a journey through the life of another person, to see some part of the world through another's eyes. We can, as a result, come to understand what it is like to live the life of a slave, a farmer, a textile worker, an engineer, a poet, a president—in a sense, to walk in another's shoes. Such experience can be personally invaluable. We cannot ask for a better entry into historical studies.

Although our personal lives are likely not as full as those we are reading about, there will be in most biographical accounts many common experiences. As with the principal character of any biography, we are also faced with numerous decisions, large and small. In the midst of living our lives we are not usually able to comprehend easily the significance of our daily decisions or grasp easily their many possible consequences, but we can gain important insights into them by seeing the decisions made by others play themselves out. We can learn from others.

Because biography is a personal story, it is almost always full of surprises. So often, the personal lives of individuals we come across historically are out of view, their public personas masking who they are. It is through biography that we gain access to their private lives, to the acts that define who they are and what they truly care about. We see their struggles within the possibilities and limitations of life, gaining insight into their beliefs, the ways they survived hardships, what motivated them, and what discouraged them. In the process we can come to understand better our own struggles.

As you read this biography, try to place yourself within the subject's world. See the events as that person sees them. Try to understand why the individual made particular decisions and not others. Ask yourself if you would have chosen differently. What are the values or beliefs that guide the subject's actions? How are those values or beliefs similar to yours? How are they different from yours? Above all, remember: You are engaging in an important historical inquiry as you read a biography, but you are also reading a literature that raises important personal questions for you to consider.

An illustration for Edgar Allan Poe's "Imp of the Perverse" represents the line of prose "There is no passion in nature so demoniacally impatient, as that of him who, shuddering upon the edge of a precipice, thus meditates a plunge."

1

The Imp of the Perverse

ON A COLD, BLUSTERY DAY at the end of February 1837, Edgar Allan Poe arrived in New York City. Although not yet famous, this man of 28 years attracted attention even on New York's busy streets. His deep-set black eyes were hypnotic, and his proud bearing, despite his tattered clothing, demonstrated an impressive self-assurance. Tucked safely among his few belongings was the reason for this man's confidence—a collection of his own stories, poems, and essays, representing more than a decade of hard work and sacrifice.

With Poe was his wife, Virginia, and his mother-in-law, Maria Clemm. They, too, probably attracted a few curious stares from passersby. Having just arrived from the small southern city of Richmond, Virginia, the two women were not dressed for the frigid winter weather, and both were taken aback by New York's hectic pace. In 1837, New York was home to more than 250,000 people, compared with Richmond's mere 20,000 residents.

Poe had deep-set, hypnotic eyes. Although his clothing often looked ragged, Poe had a proud and confident demeanor.

Virginia, then just 14 years old, was a plump young girl with a timid demeanor, whereas her mother had a stocky build and a strong-willed, independent nature. But whatever their differences in temperament, both of them were deeply devoted to the man who walked between them as they gingerly made their way north to Greenwich Village from the downtown docks.

The moody writer, in turn, was dedicated to his companions. Virginia, whom he always called "Sis," and Mrs. Clemm, his "Muddy," were practically the only family Poe had left. His foster father, John Allan, had died a few years earlier, thereby ending a difficult, often bitter relationship between the two men. In fact, although Poe had been raised by John and his wife, Frances, since the age of two, the struggling writer had not even been mentioned in the wealthy merchant's will.

Poe's real parents, two dedicated but indigent actors, had left him an orphan in 1811. It was from these troubled, creative people that Edgar Allan Poe inherited both his fertile imagination and tempestuous nature. His father, David Poe, was an alcoholic given to fits of temper and despair. His mother, Elizabeth, a remarkably talented young actress, was stricken with tuberculosis at the age of 24. Poe's memories of his mother, who died a painful death on a straw mattress in a cold room in Richmond, haunted him for the rest of his life.

"The death of a beautiful woman is, unquestionably, the most poetical topic in the world," Poe later wrote in his essay "Theory of Composition." He goes on to write: "And equally is it beyond doubt that the lips best suited for such a topic are those of a bereaved lover." In addition to his mother, Poe's very first love died at a young age. And even now, Virginia, his child-wife, displayed the fevered flush of tuberculosis on her cheeks. The themes of everlasting love, gruesome death, and bottomless grief that run through most of Poe's stories and poems were expressions of the writer's own bitter experience and deep-seated fears.

Poe, who waged a seemingly endless struggle against despair, was ill suited for the practical world. He lived on the edge of utter poverty, always owed money, and was incapable of holding a job for very long.

The ambitious young writer was not averse to hard work, however. He had already published three books of poetry and an award-winning short story. He was also an insightful editor and critic. As editor of Richmond's prestigious journal the *Southern Literary Messenger*, Poe wrote 86 reviews, 6 poems, 4 essays, and 3 stories during the year of his editorship. It was largely because of his talents that the journal's circulation rose from 500 to 3,500 subscribers in that period.

Poe's dark side often intruded upon his success. Later, he would write a story, "The Imp of the Perverse," about his tendency to do impulsively what good sense told him not to do. For Poe, that usually meant picking up a glass of liquor. Often, when he became overwhelmed by despair or frustration, he would drink too much. These excesses would leave him ill for days and unable to work.

Unfortunately, these lapses did not go unnoticed by his employers, including Thomas White, the owner of the *Messenger*. A few months earlier, White had warned Poe that his drinking was interfering with his duties as editor, but Poe was unable to control himself. It was not the first time, or the last, that Poe would lose a job on account of a bottle of wine or whiskey.

Losing the editorship of the *Messenger* was not the only reason Poe left Richmond to come north. He was anxious to fulfill his dream of owning and editing his own journal—a publication that he hoped would bring the best of American writing to the world. Poe was extremely impatient with the current literary scene. He felt there were too many second-rate writers being published by journals with low standards—and being read by an indiscriminating public. Poe was unwilling to compromise his own ideals, and his reviews of other authors' books were often savage, earning him enemies among the very people who could best help his career.

Nevertheless, Poe was gaining a reputation for his remarkable talents. When he had decided to move to New York, he was offered the chance to help develop a new journal called the *New York Review*. Its editor, Dr. Francis Hawks, agreed with Poe's assessment of the contemporary literary scene and wanted to give him a chance to cut it down to size. In a letter to Poe he wrote: "I wish you to fall in with your broad-axe amidst this miserable literary trash that surrounds you. I believe you have the will and I know you have the talent."

Consequently, Poe and his family, with hardly a penny to spare, made their way through the bustling streets of New York to a rooming house on the corner of Waverly Place and Sixth Avenue in Greenwich Village. There they would stay temporarily. As soon as they found a permanent home, Maria Clemm planned to take in boarders to supplement the family income. In the meantime, they would manage somehow. Poe was expecting some income from the last contributions he had made to the *Messenger*, and in his satchel were three new chapters of his latest and longest piece of fiction, *The Narrative of Arthur Gordon Pym*, which he hoped to sell. And he would, of course, earn income from his job as contributing editor of the *Review*.

It was with optimism, then, that Poe, his wife, and Mrs. Clemm unpacked their few belongings on that cold February day in 1837. They were welcomed to their new home by a fellow boarder, William Gowans, a bookseller who owned a shop a few blocks away at 160 Broadway. Gowans promised to introduce Poe to the many writers living in the neighborhood, some of whom were people Poe had corresponded with from Richmond. A few things seemed to be falling into place for the young author and his family.

When Poe was just 21 years old, he wrote to his foster father that he expected to spend his entire life "in indigence and sickness." Too often that statement proved to be an accurate prophecy. Even as Poe and his new friend Gowans sat down together to discuss the latest trends in literature, unseen forces were working against Poe's current plans: The panic of 1837, which would collapse the world's financial markets and disrupt all aspects of publishing, was about to begin.

No matter what obstacles Poe faced, however, he never stopped writing. The finely crafted sentences and extravagant plot lines would continue to flow from his pen, even as he suffered. "To dream," wrote Poe in one of his stories, "to dream has been the business of my life."

When Poe and his wife and mother-in-law arrived in New York City in the winter of 1837, the city probably looked very much like it does in this 1829 illustration.

2

Born in a Trunk

EDGAR ALLAN POE WAS BORN on January 19, 1809, to two struggling actors, David and Elizabeth Poe, in a run-down rooming house in Boston, Massachusetts. The Poes were so poor that they were unable to care for their firstborn son, William Henry, who was being raised by his paternal grandparents in Baltimore, Maryland. At the time of Edgar's birth, Elizabeth may have already contracted tuberculosis; David was succumbing to the ravages of alcoholism.

Although their circumstances seem to suggest otherwise, the Poes were well known in theatrical circles as hardworking, accomplished actors. As members of the Boston and Charleston Players, a prominent theatrical company, Elizabeth played leading roles in dramas by Shakespeare and other noted playwrights; David concentrated on minor dramatic parts.

Elizabeth was all too familiar with the hard lot of an actor. Because both her parents had been stars on the London stage, Elizabeth's first memories were probably of the musty smells of well-worn costumes, the glare of the footlights, and the constant travel that was a necessary part of life in the theater. Six years after her father, Henry Arnold, died in the winter of 1790, her mother, Elizabeth, decided to leave London for new challenges in the United States.

Elizabeth was just nine years old when she and her mother sailed across the Atlantic aboard the *Outram*, which landed in Boston Harbor on January 3, 1796. Several other emigrating actors were on board, including one Charley Tubbs. Tubbs became Elizabeth Arnold's second husband, either just before they left London or, more likely, soon after they arrived in the United States.

Mr. and Mrs. Tubbs appeared with considerable success in a Boston playhouse for a time and then took Elizabeth with them as they toured New England with a theater company. In Portland, Maine, young Elizabeth made her stage debut in a small part in a Gothic melodrama called *The Mysteries of the Castle*. Her first important role came a few months later, in November, when she played Biddy Bellair, a precocious young girl, in the farce *Miss in Her Teens*. Biddy Bellair quickly became one of Elizabeth's favorite roles, one she played again and again with great success.

Both Elizabeth and her mother delighted audiences and critics alike. The enthusiastic applause and the favor of the critics did not, however, translate into higher wages. Even actors with genuine talent like Elizabeth and her mother were paid a pittance for their work; most actors lived a hand-to-mouth existence, barely able to pay for food, clothing, and lodging. Acting was largely considered an unrespectable, even immoral, occupation, especially in New England, where puritanical values were firmly entrenched.

In 1797, hoping for a more congenial setting, the Tubbs family joined a theater company touring the southern states. According to a playbill, the entire Tubbs family appeared in a reading and concert in Norfolk, Virginia, on

May 2, 1798, but after this event, no further record of
Elizabeth and Charley Tubbs has been found. It is likely
they fell victim to the yellow fever epidemic that raged in
Charleston, South Carolina, that year. Elizabeth was left
an orphan at the tender age of 11.

In the late spring or early summer of 1798, Elizabeth
Arnold traveled with friends of her parents to Philadelphia,
where she joined the Virginia Players, a dramatic company
that toured the eastern United States. During the summer
season of 1801, at the age of 14, Elizabeth took the stage
as Ophelia in Shakespeare's play *Hamlet*; Shakespearean
parts would become a mainstay of Elizabeth's repertoire.

Sometime between June 12 and August 11, 1802, Elizabeth Arnold and a comedic actor named C. D. Hopkins
were married. After their marriage, the couple continued
to tour with the Virginia Players, performing in Alex-
andria, Norfolk, Petersburg, and Richmond. About three
years later, on October 26, 1805, C. D. Hopkins died after
a brief illness, leaving 18-year-old Elizabeth a widow.

Elizabeth did not remain alone for long, however. In
April 1806, she married David Poe, Jr., a dark-haired,
passionate 20-year-old actor who had joined the company
in 1804. One of David Poe's first roles was playing opposite Elizabeth in the melodramatic comedy *Speed the
Plough*; he may well have fallen in love with his beautiful
leading lady before C. D. Hopkins died.

The young man who had won Elizabeth's heart was born
in Baltimore, Maryland, and had been raised far from the
footlights of the theater. He was the son of a revolutionary
war hero, also named David, who was nicknamed the
"General" after he became the assistant deputy quarter-
master general for the city of Baltimore in 1779. He and
his wife, Elizabeth Cairnes, had seven children together;
David, Jr., born on July 18, 1784, was their eldest son. Of
their other children, only their daughter, Maria, born
in 1790, would play an important role in Edgar Allan
Poe's life.

Little is known about David Poe, Jr.'s childhood. He was evidently well educated, because at the age of 16 or 17 he studied law in Baltimore. Although rather frail in appearance, David must have been a headstrong and adventurous young man: After acting in just a few amateur productions, he decided to forsake the law and other more conservative careers for life as a professional actor. Despite his family's harsh disapproval, David left Baltimore to join a dramatic company in Charleston, South Carolina.

David Poe made his theatrical debut on the stage of the Charleston Theater on December 1, 1803. The *Charleston Courier* reviewed his performance later in the week: "He is extremely diffident; indeed so much so that the slightest lapse in his speech throws him from the little confidence he has acquired back into his first night's trepidation." Despite his apparent stage fright and unfavorable critical notice, David was a hard worker. During his first season as a professional actor, he played 24 different roles.

In May 1804, David Poe left Charleston to join the Virginia Players in Richmond, where he met and married Elizabeth Arnold Hopkins. The couple stayed with the company until May 1806, when they went north to Boston. By October, they were employed by the Boston and Charleston Players, with whom they would remain for about three years. They opened the 1806–7 theatrical season with the show that had brought them together, *Speed the Plough*. David and Elizabeth Poe received encouraging reviews, including one by critic J. T. Buckingham, who wrote, "Mr. Poe possesses a full, manly voice, of considerable extent; his utterance clear and distinct. . . . Of the talents of Mrs. Poe we are disposed to judge favorably."

When the show opened, Elizabeth was pregnant with William Henry, her first son, who was born January 30, 1807. At some point during the spring or early summer, David and Elizabeth made a difficult decision. Pressed for money and working night and day, they decided to give custody of their son to David's parents, who could better care for the infant. David himself brought the baby to Baltimore; one can only imagine the sense of shame this proud man felt upon asking his family for help.

Although the Poes had every hope of someday earning enough money to raise William Henry themselves, their fortunes fell rather than rose during the next two years in Boston. Despite their troubles, Elizabeth apparently was enchanted by the city—during her few moments of spare time, she made several sketches of Boston's picturesque sites.

On January 19, 1809, their second son, Edgar, was born. The couple remained destitute. Elizabeth had to return to the stage just three weeks after giving birth, singing and dancing to earn money. Reluctantly, David traveled to Baltimore to ask his family for funds to help pay the cost of Edgar's birth.

According to some accounts, David's temper and pride intruded; he became drunk and ill mannered, disgracing himself in front of his family before returning to Boston. Apparently, David had his own Imp of the Perverse, for on this and other occasions he did the very thing that would work against him in the long run. It was a character trait he would pass on to his newborn son.

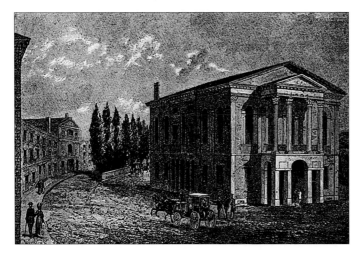

In Boston the Poes performed at such theaters as the Federal Street Theatre. Elizabeth was a highly regarded performer and played to enthusiastic audiences. David, on the other hand, was more amateurish, especially when drinking, and was rarely praised for his acting abilities.

A few months later, David and Elizabeth decided to leave Boston to seek their fortunes elsewhere. Elizabeth Poe's last appearance in Boston took place at the Exchange Coffee House on May 16, 1809. The couple then traveled to New York, where they joined the Pierce and Cooper Company at the Park Theater in September 1809. Edgar was just eight months old.

While Elizabeth played to enthusiastic audiences, David continued his downward spiral. Playbill after playbill announced that the actor was unable to perform because he was "indisposed," a euphemism for intoxicated. When he did manage to appear onstage, it was clear his alcoholism was wrecking his theatrical abilities; although never considered a great actor, he had been good enough to sustain difficult supporting roles, such as Laertes in *Hamlet* and Malcolm in *Macbeth*. After one of his last performances, however, one critic wrote, "This man was never destined for the high walks of drama; a footman is the extent of what he ought to attempt."

According to most sources, David Poe took the stage for his final performance sometime in July 1810. Exactly what happened to Edgar's father after his theater career was over is still unknown. It is likely that he remained with his wife and child for some months, although he may have deserted his family during the summer. One isolated newspaper clipping, detached and untraceable, asserts that David Poe died in Norfolk, Virginia, on October 19, 1810. However, this account has never been confirmed.

Once again, Elizabeth Poe was forced to fend for herself, this time with an infant to support and pregnant with her third child. Most disturbing of all, the cough that had once been just an annoying tickle was now waking her up at night and causing her to feel ill most of the time. In fact, Elizabeth had tuberculosis, a contagious lung disease that was slowly killing her.

With few promising prospects for work in New York, Elizabeth Poe decided to rejoin the Virginia Players. On

August 18, 1810, she opened the season of the Richmond Theater to rave reviews: "On her first moments of entrance on the Richmond Boards," wrote an enthusiastic critic, "she was saluted with the plaudits of admiration, and at no one moment since has her reputation sunk."

Once again, however, she had to leave the stage. On December 10, 1810, Edgar's sister, Rosalie, was born. Soon after the birth of her daughter, Elizabeth Poe again appeared in various roles, waging a heroic but ill-fated battle to support herself and her two infants. Beverly Tucker, a theater critic, remembered Elizabeth Poe before she was ill: "The childish figure, the great wide open, mysterious eyes, abundant curling hair confined in a bonnet . . . shadowing the brow in raven masses. . . . It is the face of an elf, a sprite." Now, however, her eyes lacked the luster that had so intrigued her audiences.

Elizabeth grew steadily more ill as she continued her tour through the South with the Virginia Players. By the time the company returned to Richmond in August 1811, she was completely exhausted. She moved into the Indian Queen Tavern, a rooming house that was owned and operated by Mrs. Phillips, a milliner who also ran a notions shop in the same building. Although she tried to continue her career, Elizabeth missed more and more performances

In 1810, Elizabeth Poe and her son Edgar had to fend for themselves. They returned to Richmond, Virginia, and in December of that year Edgar's sister, Rosalie, was born.

Frances Allan, wife of prosperous merchant John Allan, volunteered to take Edgar in and raise him when his mother died in December 1811.

as a result of her illness. At the end of October, after playing approximately 201 different roles, the hardworking actress no longer had the strength to perform.

With not a dime to their name, Elizabeth Poe and her children were completely dependent on the generosity of others for food and shelter. Fortunately, the owner of the theater company held benefits to raise money for them, announcing the events in the local newspapers. Toward the end of November, one paper appealed to its readers' charitable instincts as follows: "*To the Humane Heart*: On this night, Mrs. Poe, lingering on the bed of disease and surrounded by her children, asks your assistance and asks it perhaps for the last time."

Edgar, almost three years old, must have been confused and frightened by his mother's illness. Her fevers now gave her face an abnormal blush, and her cough racked her increasingly thin, frail body. Mrs. Phillips, as well as Elizabeth Poe's theatrical colleagues, took care of Edgar and Rosalie as the actress succumbed to her illness.

The notices about the Poes' circumstances aroused the sympathies of two well-to-do women, Frances Allan and Jane Scott Mackenzie. The wives of prosperous Richmond merchants, they visited the young family often, bringing food, blankets, and toys for the children. Knowing that she was dying, Elizabeth must have been comforted to see that Edgar and Rosalie were being cared for. In all likelihood, she believed that the children's grandfather, the General, would send for them after her death.

Finally, on December 11, 1811, Elizabeth Poe gave up her long struggle and died at the age of 24. The Richmond *Courier* printed her obituary:

> Died, on Sunday last, Mrs. Poe, one of the actresses of the company now playing on the Richmond boards. By the death of this lady, the stage has been deprived of one of its brightest ornaments and, to say the least of her, she was an interesting actress, and never failed to catch the applause and command the admiration of the beholder.

Elizabeth's orphaned children did not go to the General, after all.* Rosalie, just a year old, was adopted by Mrs. Mackenzie, and Mrs. Allan volunteered to take in Edgar. Among the little boy's few possessions was a small case containing locks of his parents' hair and a sketch of Boston Harbor, which his mother had drawn and inscribed: "For my little son Edgar, who should ever love Boston, the place of his birth, and where his mother found her best, and most sympathetic friends." Perhaps the most treasured gift from his mother was her own portrait—a miniature of her small, pert face surrounded by auburn curls. It was the only picture Edgar had of either of his parents.

With these few keepsakes, the curly-headed toddler walked with Frances Allan across Capitol Square to the home she shared with her husband, John, and her sister, Ann. What might have become of him if fate had not intervened will never be known. Two weeks later, the Broad Street Theater, where his mother would have been performing had she been alive and well, burned to the ground in a terrible fire on December 26, 1811. The governor of Virginia and 60 other people died in the fire.

Richmond's Broad Street Theatre, where Elizabeth Poe performed, burned to the ground on December 26, just two weeks after her death.

Edgar Allan Poe, depicted here in a painting by Thomas Sully, studied at the top schools while growing up. Poe often mixed with Richmond's elite and hoped to lead a life as a southern gentleman.

3

The Making of a
Southern Gentleman

FAR FROM THE AUSTERE NORTHERN CITY of his birth and even farther from the dingy rooming houses in which he had spent his first two and a half years, Edgar Poe now found himself in a genteel southern home. The Allans inhabited a spacious two-story apartment on the northeast corner of Main and Thirteenth streets, in the center of Richmond. Below their apartment was the store John Allan owned with a partner, Charles Ellis. With its colorful trinkets and rich aromas of tobacco and coffee, the busy shop, appropriately called Ellis & Allan, must have been a wonderful adventure for the young boy who had spent the last few months in his mother's sick room. Upstairs in the apartment, Edgar had his very own bedroom. There were even servants to help him wash before bed and put away his clothes.

John and Frances Allan, Edgar's new guardians, were well known in Richmond society. Although not independently wealthy, Allan was both a prosperous merchant and the potential heir to a family fortune. This status allowed the Allans to associate not only with other local merchants but with Virginia's plantation aristocracy as well.

John Allan, who ran an import-export business, did not legally adopt Edgar; however, he did allow Frances to pamper the boy.

John Allan was born in 1780 in the parish of Dundonald, Ayrshire County, Scotland. When he was 14 years old, he came to the United States to work for his uncle, William Galt, clerking in Galt's large import-export store in Richmond. Allan was ambitious and hardworking, and he learned every aspect of the business. Six years later, in November 1800, he and a fellow clerk, Charles Ellis, opened their own import-export business.

Ellis & Allan became one of Richmond's largest enterprises in the decade that followed. By 1811 the merchants were trading in a wide variety of products, including tobacco, grain, tea, coffee, wines and liquors, agricultural equipment, and hardware. They were also known to dabble in real estate, to charter ships, and to participate in the slave trade.

Three years after Ellis & Allan opened its doors, the cautious John Allan had felt his financial standing was secure enough for him to marry. On February 5, 1803, 23-year-old John Allan married 18-year-old Frances Keeling Valentine, who had moved to Richmond from Princess Anne County, Maryland. Her sister, Ann Moore Valentine, came with her and would live with the Allans throughout her life. When Edgar came into their lives eight years later, the Allans had no children of their own.

Frances Allan immediately became attached to the sweet child and did everything she could to allow Edgar to stay with her permanently. She wrote letters to the Baltimore Poes, and they responded favorably to the idea of Edgar being raised by a loving and prosperous Richmond family. General Poe, already caring for Edgar's brother, William Henry, and on a modest fixed pension from the army, lacked the resources to help his other grandchildren. Now, if Frances could only get her husband to agree, she would make all necessary arrangements with the Poes.

From the start, John Allan was ambivalent about Edgar becoming part of his family. For one thing, Allan probably had not given up hope of having his own children with his wife; he was only 31 years old, and Frances was almost 6 years younger than he. Furthermore, being a conservative businessman, he felt that even if they finally decided to adopt a child, the offspring of two impoverished actors of unknown character would not be his first choice for an heir.

Allan also had a secret: He already had a child of his own, an illegitimate son named Edward Collier. Just a few years older than Edgar, Edward also lived in Richmond, and Allan surreptitiously helped to support him and his mother. Allan was afraid, perhaps, that the two boys, so close in age, would meet someday and that Edgar would uncover Allan's secret. In fact, Allan had many love affairs that he wished to hide from his wife.

Although he never legally adopted Edgar, John Allan gave in to his wife's wishes and accepted the boy into his home. During Edgar's childhood, at least, Allan treated him as a son. From an early age, Edgar called Frances "Mama" and John "Pa."

According to the Allans' friends and neighbors, both Frances and her sister, Ann, whom Edgar called Aunt Nancy, spoiled Edgar badly. Frances especially doted on the boy, taking him with her to afternoon teas and other social events. She dressed him lavishly: One of his outfits included a purple velvet cap with a gold tassel and a crisp white blouse tucked into baggy velvet trousers. He was given his own pony to ride and puppies to play with in the yard behind the store.

Although John Allan was not as openly affectionate with Edgar, he did appear to want the very best for the youngster. To Allan, that meant a good education in Richmond's top schools. He himself was a well-read literary man who often quoted Shakespeare and other poets. When Edgar was four years old, Allan sent the child to study at a dame school, a school in which the fundamentals of reading and writing were taught by a woman in her own home. Edgar studied with a Scottish woman named Clotilda Fisher. A year later, the boy went on for lessons at a school taught by Master William Ewing.

By the time he was six, Edgar was proficient in reading, drawing, and ballroom dancing. He was quite charming and outgoing and often entertained dinner guests by reciting poetry while standing on a high-backed chair. He was also known for his mischievous pranks. His favorite trick, which was taught to him by Frances Allan's cousin, Edward Valentine, involved snatching a chair away from someone who was about to sit down. Unfortunately, Edgar's precociousness earned him more than a few spankings from his foster father. Allan was quite strict with the boy, perhaps as a counterbalance to his wife's overindulgence. But Edgar could charm even this strict taskmaster. According to Valentine, after one misadventure,

Edgar rather sheepishly, but with a grin, presented his then bemused foster father with a switch "to whip me with."

For four years after his mother's death, Edgar enjoyed a stability he had never known. Dusty stagecoach rides and long nights sleeping backstage at the theater were replaced by the comfort of a regular residence. Then, in 1815, at the age of six, he was told about his next great change of scene: traveling with the Allans across the Atlantic Ocean to England. The family would live abroad for many years so that John Allan could conduct business on behalf of his company.

Allan was going to England to try to save Ellis & Allan, which was in severe financial trouble in the aftermath of the War of 1812. The battle between England and the United States had disrupted trade between the two countries for more than three years, and Virginia tobacco merchants, such as Ellis & Allan, were especially hard hit. Many of Ellis & Allan's accounts for cargoes shipped just before the war were still outstanding. John Allan hoped that by going to England he could close out these accounts and reestablish relations with English sources.

In June 1815, Frances and John Allan, Ann Valentine, and Edgar sailed for the British Isles. About a month later, they landed in the port city of Liverpool, where they stayed for about a week while Allan sent letters to business and personal contacts in London. The family then traveled to Scotland to visit with Allan's relatives for a few months.

Once the family was ensconced in London, Edgar was sent to school, with no expense spared by Allan. It was at this time that the boy formally adopted the name Allan. At a dame school in Chelsea, where he studied for about two years, he was treated as the son of a well-to-do American merchant and was referred to in school documents as "Master Edgar Allan."

At the age of eight, Edgar was enrolled at the Manor House School, Stoke Newington, England. Later, he wrote

Edgar attended the Manor House School in Stoke Newington, England, in 1817. Reverend John Bransby, the headmaster, once said of Poe, "Edgar Allan was a quick and clever boy, and would have been a very good boy had he not been spoilt by his parents."

about his impressions of the London school in a story called *William Wilson*:

> My earliest recollections of a school life are connected with a large, rambling, Elizabethan house, in a misty-looking village of England, where a vast number of gigantic and gnarled trees stood, and where all the houses were excessively ancient. In truth, it was a dream-like and soothing place, that venerable old town.

For a boy with Edgar's imagination, the Manor House School and its surroundings must have seemed a most exotic and mysterious place indeed, especially compared with the bright, open Virginia landscape with which he was familiar.

Although his British classmates occasionally teased him about his American accent, Edgar did well at boarding school. He was especially adept at foreign languages, learning French and Latin quickly. Reverend John Bransby, the headmaster, later remembered the famous poet as a young student: "Edgar Allan was a quick and clever boy, and would have been a very good boy had he not been spoilt by his parents."

Unfortunately, John Allan's London venture did not fare well. A depression hit in 1817, causing widespread unemployment, heavy taxes, and tremendous debt both in Europe and the United States. Foreign trade remained severely restricted, and prices were fluctuating wildly. Allan wrote to his partner in Richmond to ask for money, but economic conditions were poor back home as well. The Allans remained in London for another three years, until they were forced to return to Richmond with less money and fewer prospects than they had had before leaving. On June 14, 1820, they set sail from Liverpool on the *Martha*.

The return voyage, which lasted 36 days, must have seemed a wonderful adventure to 11-year-old Edgar. By listening to tales of hurricanes and mutinies told by weather-beaten sailors and by watching as sails were hoisted and decks were swabbed, Edgar learned a great deal about life on the high seas. Years later, he would write stories about great sailing ships with a familiarity that may have stemmed from this long voyage across the Atlantic.

By midsummer 1820 the Allan family was back in Richmond. Their old apartment now rented to others and unable to afford their own home, the Allans first moved in with the Ellis family for a few months, then rented a cottage. A year later, they moved to a house owned by William Galt, John Allan's uncle.

At this time, Richmond was both a gracious southern town and a bustling state capital. Surrounded by tobacco plantations and elegant Georgian-style mansions, the city retained a genteel, rural atmosphere despite the steady influx of government employees and new businessmen. About 12,000 people lived in Richmond in 1820, about half of whom were slaves. Richmond was the seat of southern aristocracy, populated by powerful plantation owners, erudite lawyers and statesmen, and families whose wealth and social standing went back for generations.

Despite their difficult circumstances, the Allans attempted to rejoin the Richmond social scene. Allan was already at a disadvantage because he was merely a merchant, and his current financial problems only worsened his social status. Perhaps to keep up appearances as best he could, John Allan continued to send Edgar to the most expensive schools in Richmond. The sensitive young boy

Edgar and the Allans returned to Richmond in 1820. Despite its being the state capital, Richmond had a genteel, rural ambience and was surrounded by tobacco plantations and Georgian-style mansions.

found himself mixing with Richmond's elite, and he struggled hard to find acceptance among them. His foster
father's position was the least of Edgar's social problems;
his true parentage was also well known, and he endured
cruel teasing about his lowly theatrical background.

Nevertheless, Edgar made a number of friends during
his adolescence, many of whom remained loyal to him
throughout his life. For a time, he and Thomas Ellis, the
son of Allan's partner, were close friends. According to
Ellis's later recollections, Edgar's sojourn in England had
not dulled his mischievous spirit. "No one had a greater
influence over me than he had. He was indeed a leader
among his playmates; but my admiration for him scarcely
knew bounds; the consequence was, he led me to do many
a forbidden thing, for which I was punished."

Edgar's success in winning the favor of his fellow
classmates stemmed not only from his evident good humor
but from his athletic prowess as well. The years spent in
London schools, with their emphasis on physical fitness,
had turned Edgar from a slight, pale youngster into a
muscular, handsome young man. His athletic exploits became legendary. He was able to broad-jump a distance of

*An illustration from Poe's
poem "To Helen" depicts
the line "Clad all in white,
upon a violet bank / I saw
thee half reclining." Poe
was just 15 years old when
he wrote the poem to com-
memorate the death of Jane
Stanard, whom he called
Helen.*

21 feet 6 inches on a dead-level run of 20 yards. At the age of 15 he swam a distance of 7 1/2 miles against a strong tide.

Edgar continued to excel at his studies during his teen years. He became increasingly devoted to the written word, both to great literature, such as the English poets Lord Byron and John Keats, and to his own poetry and prose. William Burke, headmaster at one of Edgar's schools, recalled the boy's developing personality: "His imaginative powers seemed to take precedence over all his other faculties, he gave proof of this in his juvenile compositions, addressed to his young lady friends. He had a sensitive and tender heart."

Indeed, Edgar was particularly susceptible to the bane of adolescence—the first deep pangs of love and desire for the opposite sex. Perhaps because his mother had died so young, Poe had schoolboy crushes that were unusually intense. The earliest of his poems that survive describe the anguish and despair of adolescent love:

Oh feast my soul, revenge is sweet
Louisa, take my scorn—
Curs'd was the hour that saw us meet
The hour when we were born.

During the fall of 1823, when Edgar was 14 years old, his classmate Rob Stanard introduced Edgar to his mother, Jane Stanard, who was by all accounts a beautiful and compassionate young woman. Edgar became devoted to her. He called her Helen, which to his ears sounded far more romantic than the earthy Jane. It was to Helen that Edgar went for solace when he had problems at home or school. In many ways she became the mother he had lost so many years ago.

Tragically, Jane Stanard was dying from a malignant brain tumor. By the spring of 1824 she was confined to her bed, and Edgar was not allowed to see her. When she died on April 28, Edgar was devastated. Like his mother, she

POE'S HELEN

HELEN, LIKE THY HUMAN, EYE
THERE TH' UNEASY VIOLETS LIE—
THERE THE REEDY GRASS DOTH WAVE
OVER THE OLD FORGOTTEN GRAVE—
ONE, BY ONE, FROM THE TREE TOP
THERE THE ETERNAL DEWS DO DROP—

The lines that are on the base of Jane Stanard's gravestone are from Poe's poem "The Valley Nis."

had deserted him, dying a painful death at a young age. Helen became Edgar's ideal woman—unattainable, beautiful, and doomed. In Edgar's mind, beauty was now forever linked with death.

The loss of a trusted confidante occurred at a particularly difficult time in Edgar's life. Tensions in the Allan household had been running high for several months, since it became evident that Ellis & Allan was headed for bankruptcy. As Allan's financial situation worsened, so did his relationship with his foster son. Although Allan himself was largely responsible, he resented Edgar's fine education and the freedom he had to spend afternoons reading and writing instead of working.

Perhaps most of all, John Allan resented Edgar's attitude about life. Brought up to expect the best, Edgar did just that. When Allan's fortune declined, Edgar reacted not with compassion but with resentment and selfishness. He even complained that their modest home was not suitable to entertain his more fashionable classmates. By this time, too, Edgar probably knew of Allan's extramarital affairs and did not attempt to hide his disapproval. Indeed, Edgar's Imp of the Perverse seemed to know just the wrong thing to say to his increasingly irritable foster father.

Allan wrote about his disappointment with Edgar in a letter to William Henry Poe, Edgar's older brother, in the winter of 1824. Edgar was, he wrote, "miserable, sulky, and ill-tempered. The boy possesses not a spark of affection for us—not a particle of gratitude for all my care and kindliness to him." Edgar could not help but feel confused and betrayed by Allan's increasing coldness toward him.

The spring of 1825, however, brought an end to Allan's financial difficulties and, for a short time, to his strained relations with Edgar. In March, William Galt died, leaving his nephew a fortune of $750,000. Overnight, Allan became one of the richest men in Richmond. He then moved his family to a fashionable new address, paying nearly $15,000 for a home. The shame he had felt putting Ellis &

Allan into receivership was replaced by a new confidence and sense of security.

Edgar, too, benefited from Allan's windfall. Just when it seemed as if he would be forced to find a job as a clerk in a store, the way John Allan had at his age, Edgar was sent to a tutor to prepare for college. Allan apparently decided to enrich his obviously intelligent—if overly creative—foster son with four more years of study at the University of Virginia, which had been founded just a year before by Thomas Jefferson.

Edgar enjoyed the months before leaving for college. For the first time, he felt able to invite his wealthiest friends to his home, now sufficiently splendid. In the fall, William Henry Poe came to visit from Baltimore. The two brothers talked about literature—Henry also was an aspiring writer—and together they visited their little sister, Rosalie, who lived just a few houses away from the Allans. Twelve years old at the time of Henry's visit, Rosalie was just beginning to show signs of the mental retardation that would mark the rest of her life.

The autumn winds also brought romance into Edgar's life. He fell in love with Sarah Elmira Royster, a pretty, dark-haired girl of 15 who lived next door to the Ellis

After John Allan inherited a large sum of money upon the death of his uncle in 1825, the Allans and Poe moved into this imposing Richmond mansion. Poe benefited from his improved status within Richmond society—he was sent to a tutor to prepare for college.

family. His love was returned in full, and just before he left for college, the two proclaimed themselves engaged to be married.

At the beginning of February 1826, Edgar A. Poe, as he now called himself, traveled by stagecoach to the University of Virginia in Charlottesville. Thomas Jefferson had chosen well the site of the South's first major university, setting it in the valley between the Southwest and Blue Ridge mountains, with the Rivanna River flowing nearby its elegantly designed buildings.

Poe arrived in Charlottesville with $110 in his pocket, which Allan had given to him to cover his expenses for the entire term. But by the end of the very first day, Poe found himself already in debt. After compulsory classroom and housekeeping fees were paid, he owed more than $100— about $40 of which had to be paid immediately.

Poe wrote to Allan, explaining the situation as best he could and begging for more funds. Allan sent just $40, enough to cover Poe's immediate debt but leaving him destitute. From this time forward, the relationship between Poe and his foster father centered almost completely on money, with Poe constantly in need and Allan begrudging him every penny. Devoted to Poe, Frances tried, often in

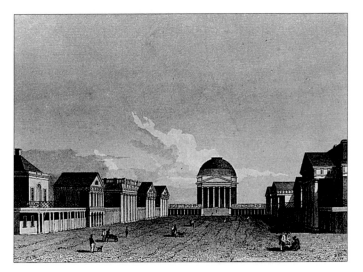

The University of Virginia in Charlottesville was founded in 1825, one year before Poe began his course of study there.

Edgar Allan Poe's name appears on an 1827 faculty record that lists the students who excelled in Latin at the University of Virginia. Poe's academic standing, however, did nothing to soothe Allan's anger over Poe's mounting gambling debts.

vain, to mend the ever-unraveling relationship between the two men in her life.

Trusting that his debts would eventually be paid, Edgar turned to the business of learning. His university schedule was not terribly demanding. Edgar was in class from about 7:00 to 9:30 A.M. every day except Sunday. On Monday, Wednesday, and Friday he studied Greek and Latin. French, Spanish, and Italian were taught on Tuesday, Thursday, and Saturday. After classes were over, students were free to do whatever they pleased.

On many afternoons, Poe sat beneath one of the huge oak trees near the university, indulging in one of his favorite pastimes: reading. He pored over every volume of Shakespeare, Milton, Dryden, Pope, Smollett, Coleridge, and Wordsworth he could find. He also enjoyed drawing, a talent he had perhaps inherited from his mother; the walls of his dormitory room were covered with crayon sketches of the surrounding countryside.

But education and solitary pursuits were not the only activities in which Edgar participated. Most of the students came from wealthy southern families and used their free time to take part in more social pastimes, such as hunting (many brought their own horses and dogs from home), drinking, and gambling. Edgar was extremely anxious to fit in with his fellow classmates at the university and joined in the festivities far too often for a young man with no money. As a consequence, he fell further and further into debt.

Gambling, however, was not Poe's only bad habit—he had a penchant for drinking. More than any other aspect of his personality, Poe's taste for alcohol has come under the greatest scrutiny from literary scholars and biographers. There can be no doubt that drinking was a problem for Edgar. It seems likely that he was alcohol-sensitive—that just one drink could make him lose control altogether. The observations of one of Poe's classmates, Thomas Tucker, support this theory:

> He would always seize the tempting glass, generally un-mixed with sugar or water—in fact, perfectly straight—and without the least apparent pleasure, swallow the contents, never pausing until the last drop had passed his lips. One glass at a time was all that he could take; but this was sufficient to rouse his whole nervous nature into a state of strongest excitement, which found vent in a con-tinuous flow of wild, fascinating talk that irresistibly enchanted every listener with siren-like power.

Throughout his life, Poe's reaction to alcohol would remain the same, often disrupting his personal and profes-sional life.

As diverting as the university's social scene was, Poe must have nevertheless studied hard, for when the term ended in December, he earned the highest distinction a student could then obtain on the final examination. Unfor-tunately, Poe's academic standing did nothing to soothe John Allan's anger. Having heard about Poe's gambling debts, Allan arrived in Charlottesville to investigate the matter himself. He was shocked to discover that his foster son owed more than $2,500 in gambling debts and personal loans. Furious, Allan paid only those he considered important and refused to pay the others. Poe was humiliated. He left for Richmond with Allan a few days later, never to return to the university.

The winter and spring of 1827 were miserable months for the shamed young man. Poe's dreams of a comfortable future as a literary scholar and writer were abruptly dashed away by Allan's consternation. Allan was angry with Poe not only for being reckless with his money but also because he had not taken any mathematics courses at school. Poe explained that he had not taken mathematics because he could not afford the tuition, but Allan did not accept this argument. He now insisted that Poe be tutored in bookkeeping and other practical trades so that he could enter the business world.

Because of the debts he owed to his classmates, Poe felt unworthy of mixing in Richmond society. Perhaps worst of all, Sarah Elmira Royster, once his beloved fiancée, refused to see him. Her father, upon hearing of Poe's misbehavior in Charlottesville from Allan, forbade the couple to meet. Poe was crushed, and he blamed his foster father for his broken heart.

Despite attempts by Frances Allan, now in poor health, to bridge the gap between her husband and her beloved foster son, the strain between the two men became overwhelming. One night in March, after a particularly bitter argument, Edgar left home. He wrote a letter to Allan from a nearby pub, stating, "[I will] now leave your house and find some place in this wide world, where I will be treated—not as *you* have treated me." He asked Allan to send him his trunk, packed with some clothes and his books, and enough money to travel north.

Perhaps thinking of his mother and the inscription she had written to him about the city of his birth, Edgar decided to head for Boston. He sailed north to New England on April 3, 1827.

An artist's depiction of a line from Poe's "Tamerlane"—"I wrapped myself in grandeur then and donned a visionary crown."

4

The Struggle Begins

EDGAR ALLAN POE ARRIVED IN BOSTON in April 1827, filled with all the indignation and pride his 18-year-old spirit could muster. He was determined to prove to his foster father, and to all those who doubted him, that he was capable of making his own way in the world. Boston was then the center of publishing, and Poe no doubt saw it as the perfect place to launch his writing career. More than anything, he wanted to become a great writer—no matter what price he had to pay. Unfortunately, Boston was not as welcoming as his mother's inscription may have led him to believe. The month Poe spent in the city was apparently a difficult one; how and where he lived are still unknown. Poe himself later told acquaintances that he spent this period in St. Petersburg, Russia, although no evidence of such a journey exists. Indeed, his penchant for fiction would often lead him to embellish the facts of his personal history.

In any event, Poe befriended a young man of about his own age named Calvin F. S. Thomas. Thomas was the proprietor of a small print shop located at 70 Washington Street in downtown Boston. Together the two men published a volume of Poe's poetry, composed during the writer's adolescent years. *Tamerlane and Other Poems* was a slender pamphlet of about 40 pages wrapped in tea-colored paper. Poe's name was not printed on the document; according to the title page, the author was simply "A Bostonian." Why Poe chose to remain anonymous is not known, but he may well have been insecure about the value of the poems included in the collection. In the introduction he wrote for the volume, he claimed he wrote the majority of poems when he was just 14 years old. He also admitted that it took courage to lay before the reading public what amounted to his life's work: "He [the author] has endeavored to expose the folly of even *risking* the best feelings of the heart at the shrine of ambition."

Poe's first published book made no impression on critical or popular readers. Only 40 or 50 copies were published, and it is doubtful that more than a handful were ever sold. Nevertheless, the poems are not without merit. They show that Poe had a remarkable sense of meter and rhythm, even as a young writer.

Although many of the poems, including the title piece "Tamerlane," concern the themes of independence, pride, and regret—typical subjects for an adolescent—there are a number that reveal Poe's already intense obsession with death. In "The Lake," Poe described the pain experienced by someone who has lost a loved one to the grave:

> In youth's spring, it was my lot
> To haunt of the wide earth a spot
> The which I could not love the less;
> So lovely was the loneliness
> Of a wild lake, with black rock bound,
> And the tall pines that tower'd around.
> But when the night had thrown her pall
> Upon that spot—as upon all,
> And the wind would pass me by
> In its still melody,

My infant spirit would awake
To the terror of the lone lake.
Yet that terror was not fright—
But a tremulous delight,
And a feeling undefin'd
Springing from a darken'd mind.
Death was in that poison'd wave
And in its gulf a fitting grave
For him who thence could solace bring
To his dark imagining;
Whose wild'ring thought could even make
An Eden of that dim lake.

"The Lake" also displays Edgar's most unique literary gift: his ability to effectively portray the often extraordinary moods evoked by ordinary places and people. Poe was not interested in simply describing the lake to the reader from an objective, realistic standpoint. Instead, he sought to characterize how the narrator of the poem was made to feel about the lake and its dark waters after his loved one died. How the human mind perceives and reacts to beauty, fear, death, and grief would become the principal subjects of Poe's writing for the rest of his career.

Unfortunately the cost of publishing the book left Poe in desperate financial straits, unemployed, and probably in debt. Rather than face the humiliation of asking John Allan for more money, the young man joined the U.S. Army. On May 26, 1827, Edgar Allan Poe enlisted under the name Edgar A. Perry. He stated his age as 22, although he was just 18. Official army documents described the writer as being five feet eight inches tall, with gray eyes, brown hair, and a pale complexion.

From May until the beginning of November, Poe lived in the barracks along Boston Harbor as a member of Battery H of the First Artillery. His regiment was then transferred to South Carolina to guard Fort Moultrie on Sullivans Island, located a few miles from the harbor at Charleston.

Private Perry, alias Edgar A. Poe, was assigned to duty as company clerk. As a member of a Coast Guard troop at a remote post during peacetime, Poe probably had a lot of free time in which to explore his new surroundings. As he strolled the beaches surrounding the fort, he luxuriated in the languid sea air and marveled at the Spanish moss hanging eerily from gnarled tree branches. Knowing the history of the island as a hideout for 18th-century pirates, Poe probably imagined pirates' galleons moored just offshore and chests filled with treasure buried beneath his feet.

Poe befriended a biologist on the island, Dr. Edward Ravenel, who helped him to appreciate the island's flora and fauna. Ravenel enjoyed describing to the curious young private the many rare types of vegetation, insects, and seashells that abounded on the island. Poe took to reading articles and books on the natural sciences, expanding his knowledge considerably.

Just as the gloomy atmosphere and Gothic architecture of London provided the mood and setting for "William Wilson" and other stories, Poe's experiences in South Carolina provided the backdrop for some of Poe's later tales, most notably "The Gold-Bug." Written in 1842, "The Gold-Bug" is a story of the search for treasure buried on Sullivans Island. The keys to finding the jewels buried long ago by the infamous pirate Captain Kidd are a map written in code and an enormous gold beetle. No doubt Poe drew inspiration for this tale from his many nature walks with Dr. Ravenel.

In addition to appreciating the South Carolina landscape, Poe was evidently excelling at his military duties. On May 1, 1828, the soldier of just less than a year earned his first promotion. Despite his success, Poe soon came to the conclusion that life as an enlisted man held no interest for him. Writing was the only thing that mattered. "I am young," he wrote in a letter to his foster father. "Not yet twenty—*am* a poet—if deep worship of all beauty can

"The Gold-Bug," Poe's story about the search for treasure buried on Sullivans Island, South Carolina, was filled with many references to his own experiences on the island while he was stationed there in the army.

make me one—and wish to be so in the more common meaning of the word. I would give the world to embody one half the ideas afloat in my imagination."

In the same letter, one of the first he wrote to Allan after nearly two years of silence, he begged Allan to help him find a way out of his five-year enlistment commitment. Allan, no doubt disappointed by what he considered another example of Poe's lack of responsibility, refused to respond.

After moving with his regiment to Fort Monroe, Virginia, Poe was again promoted, this time to sergeant major, the highest rank he could obtain without first becoming an officer. Poe wrote once more to Allan. In this letter he announced his new plan: to enter the United States Military Academy at West Point, New York, and become a military officer.

Considering that Poe already felt unsuited for the military, his decision to become an officer was most likely an attempt—albeit a dubious one—to create a respectable, steady life for himself. By becoming an officer and a gentleman, he could finally earn a place in proper society, a position that had largely been denied to him because of

Appointment to the U.S. Military Academy at West Point, New York, which is seen here as it looked in 1830, allowed Poe to get out of his enlistment commitment with the U.S. Army. Although he felt unsuited to a military career, Poe hoped he could find a respectable life for himself as an officer and a gentleman.

his lowly background as the orphaned son of two actors. And without doubt, Poe hoped he would finally win John Allan's approval and respect, as well as his financial support, by becoming an officer.

In addition, Poe felt encouraged by the assurances of a new friend and army colleague, Colonel Drayton, that his time at West Point would not be difficult. Drayton predicted that as intelligent and well educated as Poe was, the classes would not be much of a challenge for him and would leave him time to write.

Poe was still trying to convince his foster father of the wisdom of this new career when sad news reached him from Richmond. The one person he could count on to intervene with Allan, Frances, died on February 28, 1829. Granted a 10-day furlough, Poe arrived in Richmond the night after Mrs. Allan's funeral. One of her last wishes had been for the two men to reconcile. Allan had grudgingly agreed, and when Poe returned home, he gave him $50, a new suit, and whatever help he needed to enter West Point.

Back in Virginia, Poe set the wheels in motion for his discharge, enlisting the help of his regimental and company commanders, both of whom held the young man in high esteem. In addition to securing their support and Allan's permission, Poe needed to find a recruit to take his place in the regiment. Ever unlucky, especially when it came to money, Poe's substitution proved more difficult and far more costly than the usual substitution. Instead of a small fee of $10 or $20, Poe was forced to pay the much larger sum of $75 to a belligerent young sergeant named, appropriately, "Bully" Graves. Poe gave him $25 in cash and an IOU for the rest, a transaction that would soon come back to haunt him.

With glowing testimonials from all of his officers, Poe applied for admission to West Point. He took the proper documents and letters to Washington, D.C., in early May 1829, presenting them directly to Major John Eaton, the secretary of war. Told that the application process would

Major John Eaton, secretary of war, personally accepted Poe's documents when Poe applied for admission to West Point.

take several months, Poe continued on to Baltimore, Maryland, to await the results.

Poe had two reasons for visiting this city near Chesapeake Bay. Despite his implicit promise to Allan, Poe had not given up his writing career. Indeed, he had every hope of publishing another volume of poetry through one of Baltimore's many publishers.

Perhaps of more importance, however, was his desire to reestablish ties with the Poe side of his family. While in the army, his curiosity had been piqued about his grandfather, "General" David Poe, and his illustrious exploits during the revolutionary war.

Poe arrived in Baltimore in May 1829 to find his aged grandmother, General Poe's widow, living with Maria Clemm, his aunt, and with Clemm's 2 children, Henry, aged 11, and Virginia, a plump, dark-haired child of 7. Also with them was William Henry, Poe's 22-year-old brother.

If Poe, who arrived at their door nearly penniless, expected any financial help from his Baltimore relatives, he was sorely disappointed. The Clemms and Poes were even more poverty-stricken than he was himself. Nevertheless, they welcomed Edgar into their home and their hearts.

Poe did not stay with his relatives for long and instead took an inexpensive room in a nearby boardinghouse. He then set about finding a publisher for his poetry collection, to which a few new poems had been added and for which many others had been revised during his time in the army. On May 11 he called on William Wirt, a prominent lawyer and author (and former U.S. attorney general), whom Poe first met at the University of Virginia. With Wirt's help, Poe established important connections in the publishing world.

On Wirt's advice, Poe brought his manuscript to the Philadelphia firm of Lea, Carey & Lea, who refused to publish the volume of an unknown without first receiving a financial guarantee of $100. Although he tried, Poe did not obtain the money from Allan, who was somewhat shocked to find that his wayward son still clung to the idea of becoming a writer.

Undaunted, Poe then sent a selection of poems to John Neal, editor of the *Yankee & Boston Literary Gazette*, as well as to Hatch & Dunning, a Baltimore publisher. In September he received his first words of real support from an editor. Although Neal did not accept any of the poems for publication in the *Yankee*, he did publish his review of them. He judged many of Poe's poems to be "nonsense" but also claimed that the poet had much talent and might someday "make a beautiful and perhaps a magnificent poem."

Poe was further encouraged by news from Hatch & Dunning, which agreed to publish *Al Aaraaf, Tamerlane, and Minor Poems* in December. Unfortunately, Poe's

Maria Clemm, Poe's aunt, lived in Baltimore, Maryland, with her mother and her two children, Henry and Virginia. When Poe arrived at Clemm's door nearly penniless in 1829, he found that his relatives were just as poor as he was.

second volume of poetry received only slightly more attention than his first. The few critics who did review it
found many of the poems immature and confusing. The
title poem, the 400-line "Al Aaraaf," they considered to be
especially obscure. It concerned beauty (Poe's favorite
theme) and how beauty is communicated by God to people.

Nevertheless, the new poems did earn Poe a few ac-
colades; Sarah Hale, editor of the *Ladies Magazine*, wrote,
"The author, who appears to be very young, is evidently a
fine genius, but he wants judgement, experience, tact."

As lukewarm as these first reviews were, they did give
Poe a bit of respectability, at least in the eyes of the Poe
family. Poe remained in Baltimore until the end of December, when a long-awaited letter arrived from John Allan.
Edgar was invited, for the first time in many years, to return
to Richmond. He bade a temporary farewell to the Clemms
and gratefully went home.

After Maria Clemm's crowded quarters and his sparse
boardinghouse room, the spaciousness of the Allan home
must have seemed luxurious indeed. Although exactly
what occupied Poe during the winter and spring of 1830 is
unknown, it is likely that he stayed in Richmond while
awaiting news from West Point, working diligently on new
poems in his cozy, bookcase-lined room on the second
floor of the family home.

Confirmation of his appointment to the military academy came through in March, and Poe entered the academy
on July 1, 1830, hoping for a good education, increased
employment opportunities, and, of course, a chance to
prove himself to his eternally distant foster father.

Unfortunately, Colonel Drayton's assurances that the
academy's requirements would leave Poe with lots of time
to write did not prove to be the case. Cadet Poe began
classes at dawn, breakfasted at 7:00 A.M., attended classes
from 8:00 until 1:00, ate a quick lunch, then continued to
study from 2:00 to 4:00 P.M. The students then participated
in a few hours of military exercises until supper was served

at sunset. After the meal, more classes were conducted until 9:30 P.M. The cadets had just enough time to wash up and get into bed before lights-out was called at 10:00 P.M. So there were few spare hours during which Poe could write or meander along the magnificent Hudson River, which flowed past the academy.

In addition to the demanding class schedule, West Point had more than 300 rules and regulations proscribing leisure activities. Not only were drinking, smoking, and card playing prohibited, but so, too, was the reading of any novel or poem not directly related to class work. Such a rule must have deeply offended the poet. Despite his increasing dissatisfaction with West Point, Poe managed to progress there as well as he had in South Carolina. He made a number of friends among the generally younger cadets, who were amused by the satirical poems he composed about their commanding officers. He also intrigued his fellow soldiers with a grandly embellished personal history that included claims that he had spent time in Russia and that he was related to Benedict Arnold.

Although he was never caught, Poe apparently drank frequently while he was at the academy. According to Thomas Gibson, one of his roommates, Poe drank copious amounts of brandy, which he somehow managed to smuggle into their room. Whether or not Poe drank more than other men his age, however, is open to speculation. But there is no doubt that he was growing increasingly unhappy as the term wore on. Gibson, in an article he wrote in 1867, recalled Poe as he appeared at West Point: "He had a worn, weary, discontented look, not easily forgotten by those who were intimate with him."

Poe's emotional burden only increased during the fall and winter, when relations between him and John Allan further deteriorated. As usual, money was the cause of the tension, at least on the surface. Poe's unfinished business with Bully Graves, the substitute recruit in Virginia, came to Allan's attention in the spring of 1831. Hoping to collect his $50 from Allan, Graves sent the merchant a letter written by Poe the year before. In it Poe claimed that Allan had already paid the debt. If he had not, it was because "Mr. Allan is not very often sober."

Allan was furious that such a disloyal and ugly lie would be told by a young man he had supported for so many years. Although Poe apologized, the damage clearly had already been done. This incident was the last straw for Allan. He was about to start a new life by remarrying and evidently had decided to wipe his hands of Poe and his life-style once and for all.

By the time midterm exams were held in early January 1830, Poe knew that joining West Point had been a mistake. Sick with a fever and an ear infection, he wrote to Allan, begging him for help and insisting that if he did not receive it, he would get himself ejected from the academy on his own.

When Allan ignored this plea, Poe proceeded to carry out his threat. Although West Point records show that out of a class of 86 he stood third in French and 17th in mathematics, he was court-martialed on January 28, 1831. He was charged with gross neglect of duty, including absenting himself from parades, roll calls, and classes, as well as disobeying orders.

By his 21st birthday, on January 19, Poe had left West Point. Discouraged and still feverish, he made his way down the Hudson to New York City. His only consolation was that in his pocket was a subscription list circulated among his fellow students. Each of them had donated 75 cents to help pay for the publication of a new volume of poems. Poe may well have used some of this money to pay for his room and board, for there is no record of Allan's sending him any money. In fact, Allan made a note on the back of one of Poe's letters, dated from this time, describing his foster son as having "the blackest heart and deepest ingratitude."

Thanks in large part to the West Point subscription list, however, Poe was able to convince a New York publisher, Elam Bliss, to print *Poems by Edgar A. Poe, Second Edition.* A booklet of 124 pages dedicated to the "U.S. Corps of Cadets," *Poems* appeared in April 1831. It included some previously published works, such as "Tamerlane" and "Al Aaraaf," as well as new pieces, such as "To Helen," Poe's ode to his first love, Jane Stanard.

In the preface to the book, Poe paid tribute to Samuel Taylor Coleridge, an English poet and literary critic of the late 18th and early 19th centuries. Poe also discussed for the first time his own theories about the nature of art and poetry by elaborating upon Coleridge's definition of poetry.

"A poem, in my opinion," he wrote, "is opposed to a work of science by having, for its *immediate* object pleasure, not truth." Through poetry, he postulated, both the poet and the reader glimpse a beauty beyond ordinary human experience. The reactions this glimpse cause have nothing to do with logic, intellect, or conscience but rather with pure emotional ecstasy. To evoke that ecstasy, then, is the true purpose of poetry. As Poe's career continued, he would return again and again to this theme, expanding and refining his ideas about the meaning and purpose of art.

Despite the maturity of thought expressed in the preface, Poe's third volume of poetry failed to earn any attention. Discouraged and broke, the young poet left New York in the spring of 1831 and headed for the only home he felt would welcome him, that of his aunt, Maria Clemm, in Baltimore. Hearing that John Allan had married Louisa Patterson, a young woman sure to bear him legitimate heirs, Poe gave up his dream of becoming a southern gentleman. Poe now knew he belonged with his true father's family. It was with them that his struggle would continue.

This illustration from Poe's arabesque "Metzengerstein" depicts the line "Leaping with an impetuosity which outstripped the very Demon of the Tempest."

5

A Reputation Grows

IN MARCH 1831, EDGAR ALLAN POE arrived by steamship in Baltimore, which was then the third largest city in the United States, after New York and Philadelphia, and was a center of intellectual activity. According to a 1927 article published in the *Maryland Historical Magazine*, more than 70 new periodicals started up in the city between 1815 and 1833. Although most did not survive for more than a few issues, Poe was encouraged by the citizens' apparent interest in literary matters.

Poe had about a mile to walk from the busy Baltimore piers to the home of his aunt. Located in the center of the business district, on Milk Street in Mechanics Row, Maria Clemm's two-story house was home to the same struggling family Poe had met almost two years before, although now their situation was even more dire.

In the 1827 volume of *Matchett's Baltimore Directory*, Maria Clemm was listed as the "preceptress [teacher] of school, State St., North Side near Foot Bridge." But when Poe arrived in 1831, she was at home nursing his brother and grandmother and tending to the two children. The entire household, it seemed, was surviving on just $240 a year, the income from General Poe's pension.

Edgar's grandmother, Mrs. David Poe, was desperately ill, paralyzed by a stroke and requiring constant care. William Henry, Poe's older brother, was suffering from alcoholism and the last stages of tuberculosis. In fact, he died just a few months later, on August 1, 1831, at the age of 24. Maria Clemm's two young children, Henry, 13, and Virginia, 9, were given whatever love and attention their mother had left at the end of her long day.

As soon as he arrived, Poe applied for and was refused at least two jobs: one as a writer at the *Federal Gazette*, edited by William Gwynne, and one as a teacher at a school in a nearby town. As poor as ever, with no prospects for employment and having published three books that did not advance his professional standing, Poe probably felt discouraged during the spring of 1831.

Nevertheless, settling into his attic room, Edgar Poe diligently continued to do the only thing that really mattered to him: write. Although poetry would remain his

A facsimile of the introduction to "The Folio Club" from Poe's orginal manuscript. Poe wrote the stories primarily to satirize current writers and their styles.

THE FOLIO CLUB

There is a Machiavelian plot
Though every nare olfact it not
                              Butler

THE Folio Club is, I am sorry to say, a mere Junto of Dunderheadism. I think too the members are quite as ill-looking as they are stupid. I also believe it their settled intention to abolish Literature, subvert the Press, and overturn the Government of Nouns and Pronouns. These are my private opinions which I now take the liberty of making public.

creative passion, Poe began to focus his writing in a new direction, one with more money-making potential. Letting his vivid imagination loose, he started to write short stories that he hoped would sell to the many popular magazines then being published. A tempting offer posted by the *Philadelphia Saturday Review* in June no doubt encouraged Poe to pursue the short story genre. The magazine offered to pay $100 to the author of the best short story submitted by December 1, 1831.

Throughout that summer and fall Poe worked at a feverish pace, producing not one but five tales. These stories, and six others he wrote over the next few years, were known as the "Tales of the Folio Club." Because he himself was not famous—or wealthy—Poe attributed the authorship of each story to a different member of an imaginary elite literary society, the Folio Club.

Poe originally wrote the stories to satirize current writers and their styles. They fell into two categories, the grotesques and the arabesques. The grotesques were absurdly humorous tales. Indeed, although Poe became best known for his tales of horror, he also was a gifted comic writer as well. One of the early grotesques was "The Duke de L'Omelette," about a man who dies of shock at being served food improperly and who then must play a game of cards with the Devil. According to Poe biographer William Bittner, the inspiration for this tale may have been N. P. Willis, the editor of a New York journal, whose literary and personal style apparently annoyed Poe. Such jibes at prominent literary figures would later come back to haunt their author.

Poe's arabesques were tales of terror modeled largely on the works of German horror writer E. T. A. Hoffmann. But instead of creating humorous parodies, Poe found himself able to evoke honest dread and terror once he began to write. In fact, by expressing his emotions, fueled as they were by his difficult past, Poe gave these fantastic tales a dark, compelling sincerity.

One of the arabesques, called "Metzengerstein," remains one of Poe's most popular tales. It is the story of Baron Metzengerstein, a young man of 15, who kills Count Berlifitzing, an old family rival. The figure in a tapestry that hung over his mantel then comes to life, releasing into the real world a wild horse possessed by the spirit of the dead count. When the young baron rides the horse, both horse and rider die in a fiery blaze created by their own hatred for each other.

Although most literary scholars agree that "Metzengerstein" is not one of Poe's best works, it demonstrates one of his greatest strengths as a writer: the ability to so convincingly create a world filled with totally unnatural events—such as a tapestry coming to life—that a reader is moved by all of the emotions evoked by the story's characters and events. The reader feels not just amazement and fear but loneliness, hatred, and grief as well.

At the end of November 1831, Poe mailed five stories to Philadelphia. Although none of the stories won the $100 prize, the judges enjoyed them enough to publish each of them during the following year. Although Poe no doubt was pleased to see his work in print, it is unlikely that he received a penny for all his hard work. Adding insult to injury, neither was he credited with the authorship of the stories. According to contemporary literary practices, the works appeared unsigned in the magazine.

In the meantime, Poe was getting to know some of his literary colleagues in Baltimore. One of his closest friends during this period was writer-editor Lambert Wilmer, who worked for the local journal the Baltimore *Saturday Visitor*. Equally poor and struggling, the two men shared the same dream: to own and edit their own magazine that would feature only the best, most original American literature. Poe's ambition evidently was backed by a stringent work ethic. "He appeared to me," Wilmer later reminisced, "to be one of the most hardworking men in the world. I called to see him at all hours, and always found him employed."

In the moments Poe was not writing, he was enjoying the company of his family. There were a number of Poes still living in Baltimore, including cousins Neilson Poe and Rebecca Herring, Maria Clemm's niece, with whom Poe apparently had a brief flirtation. Since his brother's death, Poe spent more and more time with his cousin Virginia, who was blossoming into a charming young woman. With her dark hair, pale skin, and bright eyes, Virginia may well have reminded Poe of his own mother.

Poe's need for family, for a sense of security and unconditional love that he had never had before, was deep and grew deeper as his relationship with Allan deteriorated. He no longer communicated with Allan at all, except when his financial situation was especially desperate. Poe usually received no reply; only occasionally would Allan respond by sending money.

Most of the following year, 1833, was as bleak as any Poe had yet lived. On what funds the family survived is unknown. Nevertheless, the ambitious author remained undaunted. After finishing his "Tales of the Folio Club," he set about finding a publisher for them. Poe's rather grim financial situation was made clear by the postscript to the letter he sent with the manuscript to *New England Magazine* that read, "P.S. I am poor."

On June 15 a ray of hope appeared in the form of a new contest, this one sponsored by the Baltimore *Saturday Visitor*, offering $50 for the best short story and $25 for the best poem submitted by October 1. Poe entered a new poem, called "The Coliseum," and six Folio Club stories.

On October 12 the judges announced their decision. "MS. Found in a Bottle" written by Edgar A. Poe was by far the best story submitted. (*Ms.* is an abbreviation for *manuscript.*) Like many of his other Folio Club tales, this one starts out to be a satire of the sea stories that were

Poe won a $50 prize for his short story "MS. Found in a Bottle." An illustration from the story represents the line "We are plunging madly within the grasp of the whirlpool—and amid a roaring, and bellowing, and thundering of ocean and tempest, the ship is quivering—oh God! and—going down!"

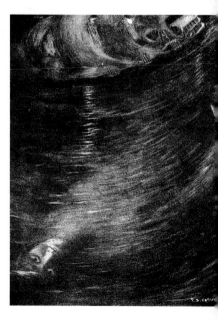

John Pendelton Kennedy, one of the judges for the Saturday Visitor'*s writing contest, later became a friend of Poe's. With Kennedy's help Poe landed a job with the* Southern Literary Messenger.

hugely popular at the time. But Poe's remarkable writing skills turn the tale—about a ship that grows as if it is a living thing—into an intricately detailed adventure that effectively mixes the natural and supernatural.

In announcing the winning story, the judges also highly recommended all six of Poe's submissions: "These tales are eminently distinguished by a wild, vigorous, and poetical imagination, a rich style, a fertile invention, and varied and curious learning." In many ways, these words meant more to Poe than the much-needed $50. They meant he had gained a measure of respect from Baltimore's literary elite. Hoping to take advantage of his new standing, he contacted the judges who enjoyed his work.

John Latrobe was the first to receive a visit from Poe. Forty-four years later, Latrobe recalled the 1833 meeting, painting a vivid and valuable picture of the author: "His figure was remarkably good, and he carried himself erect and well, as one who had been trained to it. He was dressed in black, and his frockcoat was buttoned to the throat, where it met the black stock. Not a particle of white was visible." Latrobe went on to say that although Poe's clothes were tattered and worn, the author had clearly tried to make them presentable. "On most men his clothes would have looked shabby and seedy, but there was something about this man that prevented one from criticizing his garments."

Another contest judge, John Pendleton Kennedy, then 38 years old and a respected lawyer in Baltimore, also met Poe that autumn, and the two became friends. Kennedy, a novelist himself, would be an important source of friendship, financial support, and professional encouragement to Poe for many years. He immediately set about finding work for his brilliant, but obviously needy, new friend. His help came just in time.

During the winter of 1834, Poe received word from Richmond that John Allan was dying. According to an account given by the second Mrs. Allan, Poe made one last, disastrous visit to his foster father. Louisa Allan claimed that Poe, drunk and disheveled, burst into Allan's bedroom. Allan then shook his cane at Edgar, who abruptly left the room without speaking a word. Allan died a few weeks later, on March 17, 1834.

Although Louisa Allan might have exaggerated the hostility of the encounter, John Allan's feelings about Edgar Poe were made evident upon the reading of his will. While providing for his immediate family, as well as for his illegitimate children, John Allan did not so much as mention Edgar Allan Poe's existence. The final blow in the 25-year battle of wills thus was struck, devastating the young author, who had wanted nothing more than approval and support from the only father he had ever known.

It was not until the following year that Poe's seemingly endless run of bad luck began to change. After an introduction from his friend John Kennedy, Poe began a correspondence with Thomas White, the owner of the *Southern Literary Messenger*. Located in Richmond, Virginia, Poe's old hometown, the *Messenger* was the South's most important literary journal.

During the winter and spring of 1835, White published several of Poe's short stories, including "Berenice" and "Morella." Both concern Poe's primary obsession: the death of a beautiful woman and the power of love and beauty to survive beyond the grave. Although he wrote his stories to appeal to fans of the horror-story genre that was currently popular, they were written with a poetic passion that raised them far above the average potboiler.

In "Morella," a dead woman's spirit is reincarnated in the body of her daughter when her husband names the child after her, calling her Morella during the baptism. The horrified husband and father looks on:

> What fiend spoke from the recesses of my soul, when, amid those dim aisles, and in the silence of the night, I shrieked within the ears of the holy man the syllables— Morella? What more than fiend convulsed the features of my child, and overspread them with the hues of death, as,

An illustration of a line from "Morella": "And thus joy suddenly faded into horror, and the most beautiful became the most hideous." The story concerns Poe's primary obsession: the death of a beautiful woman.

starting at that scarcely audible sound, she turned her glassy eyes from the earth to heaven, and, falling prostrate upon the black slabs of her ancestral vault, responded—"I am here."

Evidently appreciating the remarkable talent such writing conveyed, Thomas White wrote to Poe in June and offered him a job. Like many magazine owners of the time, White was a printer, not an editor, and required someone with literary taste and editorial talent to run his journal. Although Poe still harbored dreams of owning his own magazine, the need for a salary and the allure of an editor's position prompted him to accept White's offer.

Sometime during the summer of 1835, Poe left the Clemm household to return to Richmond and begin work at the *Messenger*. The homecoming was a difficult one, and despite his new job, he almost immediately fell into a deep depression. He was haunted by memories of the past and frustrated by his dashed dreams of becoming a southern gentleman. Most of all, he missed his new family back in Baltimore.

In fact, Poe had formed a deep attachment not only to the motherly Maria Clemm but to her daughter, Virginia, as well. Over the years, Virginia had come to embody Poe's ideal woman: pale, dark haired, and infinitely devoted to him. He first realized the depth of his feeling for her when he received a letter from Maria Clemm, announcing that Neilson Poe had offered to take Virginia in and pay for her education. Poe wrote back to Mrs. Clemm, declaring his love for her daughter.

The question of whether Poe was in love with Virginia in a romantic or sexual sense has never been answered. That he was completely devoted to her, however, there is no doubt. A clue to his feelings for her may be found in his story "Morella," in which the author wrote:

. . . fate bound us together at the altar; and I never spoke of love, nor thought of passion. She however, shunned society, and, attaching herself to me alone, rendered me happy. It is a happiness to wonder;—it is a happiness to dream.

The need for such emotional security motivated Poe to cling to Virginia, and the idea of her leaving Baltimore drove him to distraction that summer.

Overwhelmed by loneliness and frustration, Poe drank to excess night after night. It was the first time in many years that he had overindulged in alcohol; it was a habit his system still could not tolerate. His bouts would leave him sick for days, unable to work, unable to write, and in the deepest despair.

Within a few months of his arrival, Edgar Poe was fired, at least temporarily, from his first editorial position. Not surprisingly, he returned immediately to Baltimore, to Maria Clemm and his beloved Virginia. He knew then what he must do to remain tied to this earth and not be lost to madness and gloom. On September 22, 1835, he applied for a license to marry his cousin. They officially married about a year later.

More good fortune followed. At the end of September 1835, a letter from Thomas White arrived from Richmond. Writing in a fatherly tone, White expressed his regret at firing Poe and offered to rehire him—if Poe promised never to drink again. The magazine owner went on to praise Poe's literary talents but cautioned the young man about the dangers of alcohol. "No man is safe who drinks before breakfast," White wrote, and if Poe were to drink again, he would be fired at once.

With firm resolve never to take another sip of alcohol, Poe returned to Richmond. This time, Maria Clemm and Virginia were with him. They now had only each other: Mrs. Clemm's son, Henry, had gone off to sea, and Mrs. David Poe, Poe's grandmother, had passed away in July. Poe and the two women in his life moved into a boardinghouse on the corner of Twelfth and Bank streets on Capitol Square.

Virginia Clemm embodied Poe's image of the ideal woman—she was pale, dark haired, and forever devoted to him.

The next year was perhaps the happiest Poe had yet experienced. Although he still struggled financially— White paid him just $15 per week—he had both a family who loved him and a job that suited his abilities. With energy and purpose he worked diligently to make the *Messenger* a first-rate publication.

In addition to reprinting some of his stories and poems, Poe expanded his skills in yet another direction, one that would allow him to have a considerable impact on the world of American letters. He became one of the first true literary critics in the United States, reviewing dozens of novels and poems in the *Messenger*.

Poe's marriage license is dated May 16, 1836. Although the license states that Virginia Clemm was 21 years old, at the time she was only 14.

In 1942, Edmund Wilson, one of the 20th century's foremost literary critics, praised Poe's talent as a critic when he wrote, "Intellectually, he stands on higher ground than any other American writer of his time." Wilson went on to describe three major goals he felt Poe undertook through his criticism.

First, Poe wanted to feature only the best of American literature and had no misgivings about criticizing what he considered poor writing—no matter who the author was. In this he differed from many of his fellow American critics, who often recommended a work simply because an American had written it. On the other hand, he was fighting another tendency in America to overinflate the importance and quality of *British* writers and critics. Just because a novel or poem was published in London, Poe insisted, did not necessarily mean it was great literature.

Poe's third goal was perhaps his most important: to break down the regional barriers within the United States. At the time, New England was considered the capital of intellectual activity in the United States. Writers such as Henry Wadsworth Longfellow and Ralph Waldo Emerson, Poe felt, formed a kind of clique that kept out southerners and, for a time, New Yorkers. He took every opportunity to attack the conservative and provincial New England writers.

In attempting to accomplish such lofty goals, Poe set his standards for literature and poetry quite high, and few works measured up to them. Moreover, because his reviews were not meant as constructive criticism but rather as treatises about standards of literature, they were often scathing. Although most authors reviewed by Poe probably deserved the bad notices—few of their works have survived to be read by future generations—Poe managed to make many enemies through his early reviews.

Although the *Messenger*'s circulation increased more than tenfold under Poe's editorial direction, Thomas White became increasingly uncomfortable with the way Poe was

Maria Clemm's house on Carmine Street was Poe's first real home in New York City. While the hardworking Poe continued his writing, Clemm took in boarders to help earn money.

handling his job. Not only were Poe's controversial essays offending some of White's best customers, but in White's opinion, Poe was trying to run the magazine as if it were his own. Worst of all, it appeared that Poe had broken his solemn vow. He was drinking again.

Finally, in the fall of 1836, White felt he had to fire Poe once and for all. "Highly as I really think of Mr. Poe's talents," he wrote to a friend in December, "I shall be forced to give him notice in a week or so at the farthest that I can no longer recognize him as editor of my *Messenger*."

In many ways Poe was relieved his relationship with the *Messenger* was over. He was pitifully underpaid for the amount of work he performed, and he neither trusted nor respected Thomas White. And although Poe had become somewhat known as a critic in the South through his work at the *Messenger*, he knew that to achieve true fame for his own writing he must establish a reputation in New York, Philadelphia, or Boston, the major literary centers in 19th-century America.

Thanks to his dismissal by White, Poe was ready to take his experience and exceptional talent north. His first stop was New York City, where work had been offered to him at the *New York Review*. The Poe family arrived in the bustling city in February 1837. Unfortunately, because of a national financial crisis, the *Review* and most other magazines were forced to suspend publication for a number of months. In addition, Poe's harsh criticisms had indeed earned him a few enemies among the New York literati, who may have been unwilling to hire him even if work had been available.

Poe struggled through a difficult year, surviving only with the help of Maria Clemm, who took in boarders to earn a little money. Poe diligently continued to write, completing his longest work, *The Narrative of Arthur Gordon Pym*, which he sold to Harper's publishing company. The story of a stowaway's adventures on a whaling ship, *Pym* drew on Poe's personal knowledge of the sea. It also drew on his understanding of the public's appetite for such tales, evidenced by the continued popularity of *Robinson Crusoe*, published in 1719 by Daniel Defoe. However, Poe was again disappointed by the lack of critical or popular notice of his new book.

Although his literary experiences in New York were not successful, Poe did not give up his struggle for recognition. Packing up once again, he, his wife, and his mother-in-law headed to Philadelphia. After working so long and hard without any apparent reward for his labors, Poe was about to embark on the most successful and creative period in his life.

Poe sold The Narrative of Arthur Gordon Pym, *a story about a stowaway's adventures on a whaling ship, to Harper's publishing company. This picture illustrates a line from the story: "On his back there sat a huge sea gull busily gorging itself with the horrible flesh."*

In Philadelphia the Poes and Maria Clemm lived in this six-room house at 530 North Street. Poe wrote some of his most popular stories, including "William Wilson," "The Gold-Bug," and "The Fall of the House of Usher," in Philadelphia.

6

At the Summit

LIKE HIS PARENTS BEFORE HIM, Edgar Allan Poe seemed destined to travel from city to city in order to make his mark: first to Boston, then to Baltimore, back to Richmond, then on to New York, and now to Philadelphia. He had been married for just two years, yet his new family had already lived in three different cities.

The difficulties the Poe family experienced in Richmond and New York had taken their toll on Virginia. Now 16 years old, the dark-haired, plain-faced young woman was already beginning to show signs of illness. Although still a bit plump, she was physically frail and tired easily. It was her mother, in fact, who did most of the housekeeping chores and cooking. Indeed, although Virginia provided her husband with inspiration and devotion, it was 47-year-old Maria Clemm who formed the stable center of the struggling author's life.

The first year the family spent in Philadelphia was as difficult as the one just passed in New York. Although the city shared the honor with New York as a center of publishing, Poe had trouble selling his stories to the city's many magazines. In fact, his most important work of 1838, a story called "Ligeia," was sold to the Baltimore journal *American Museum*, owned by two former acquaintances of Poe's, Nathan Brooks and J. E. Snodgrass. Like "Morella" and "Berenice," "Ligeia" is the tale of a beautiful woman who dies at a young age. Although considered one of Poe's best stories, even by the author himself, he was paid only $10 for it.

Besides "Ligeia," Poe managed to publish several other stories in the *American Museum*, including "The Psyche Zenobia" and "The Scythe of Time," burlesque satires of stories made popular in the English magazine *Blackwood's* and elsewhere. Although Poe was quite productive during his first year in Philadelphia, his publishing successes did not earn him much money. In order to support his family, he agreed to take on a project that would later tarnish his reputation.

Sometime during the fall of 1838, Poe was asked by the author and scientist Thomas Wyatt to prepare a book on shells and mollusks called *The Conchologist's First Book*. For this project Poe merely wrote an introduction and made some minor changes to a book already published by Wyatt himself and to a textbook written by a French scientist named Cuvier. The title page of the textbook, however, listed only Edgar A. Poe as the author, with a minor credit to Cuvier. Although Poe freely admitted his limited role in the book, he would later be accused of plagiarism. It was ironic, however, as noted by Poe biographer Arthur Hobson Quinn, that this book on shells was probably the only volume by Poe that went into a second edition during the author's lifetime.

As the summer of 1839 approached, Poe, still in need of money, decided to join the staff of a Philadelphia journal called *Burton's Gentlemen's Magazine*. *Burton's* was owned and run by William E. Burton, an English actor who was publishing the magazine in order to raise money to start his own theater in Philadelphia.

William E. Burton, an English actor who founded the Philadelphia journal called Burton's Gentlemen's Magazine, *hired Poe to work for his publication in 1839.*

A more direct opposite in personality to the serious, often melancholy Poe could not be found. William Burton was a loud, frequently rambunctious man who, by nature, insisted on controlling every aspect of his magazine. Whereas Poe still dreamed of a top-notch literary journal, Burton intended his magazine to be a money-making vehicle featuring popular entertainment. Indeed, he warned Poe that the author's high standards and harsh criticisms of other writers would not be tolerated.

Despite their obvious differences, the two men made an agreement: Poe would be paid $10 a week for what Burton supposed would be about 2 hours per day of writing and editorial work. As usual, however, Poe put in more than his share of time and energy. The first issue to which he contributed included five pages of his criticism and two previously published, but newly revised, poems.

Ignoring Burton's warning, Poe continued to write critical essays with a rather stern tone. In the July issue, his leading review concerned James Fenimore Cooper's work of nonfiction, *The History of the Navy*. Although Poe praised the book, he referred to Cooper's other recent work as "a flashy succession of ill-conceived and miserably executed literary productions, each more silly than its predecessor." Although most critics agree that Cooper's books from this period were not his best, Poe again had attacked one of America's leading men of letters.

In the same issue, he reviewed a poem by his old friend from Baltimore, Lambert Wilmer. He praised the poem's composition, but nevertheless used the review to poke fun at some of America's most established literary figures. "Mr. [William Cullen] Bryant is not *all* a fool. Mr. [N. P.] Willis is not *quite* an ass. Mr. [Henry Wadsworth] Longfellow *will* steal, but, perhaps, he cannot help it."

This criticism of Longfellow sowed the seeds of a long and bitter feud between the authors. Just a few months later, Poe reviewed Longfellow's new poem, *Voices of the Night*, which he declared lacked the unity of tone that

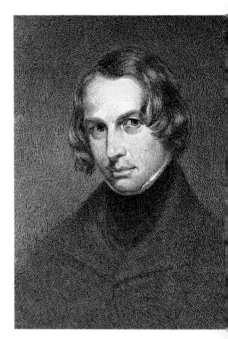

The poet Henry Wadsworth Longfellow was frequently a target of Poe's biting literary criticism. Poe accused Longfellow of plagiarizing Alfred, Lord Tennyson.

formed the basis of decent poetry. He also accused the poet of plagiarizing Alfred, Lord Tennyson, an absurd charge by all accounts.

It must be said that Poe did not write these reviews solely to strike at more established authors. Behind his cutting remarks lay a deeply held and well-considered philosophy of literature. That Poe lacked the tact to phrase his ideas in a more benevolent manner contributed greatly to his professional difficulties, especially as his career progressed.

In September, Poe presented the magazine with one of his greatest stories, "The Fall of the House of Usher." From the opening page of this tale of madness and decay, Poe established a mood of terror and mystery through the eyes of the narrator:

> I looked upon the scene before me,—upon the mere house, and the simple landscape features of the domain—upon the bleak walls—upon the vacant eye-like windows—upon a few rank sedges—and upon a few white trunks of decayed trees—with an utter depression of soul which I can compare to no earthly sensation more properly than to the after-dream of the reveller upon opium.

Within the decaying house lived Roderick Usher and his twin sister, Madeline, both of whom were wasting away from some unknown illness. Roderick admits to the narrator his belief that the house itself is a malevolent being possessing their bodies and causing them to disintegrate. The themes of loss of identity and of madness were also explored in another of Poe's tales composed in 1839, "William Wilson," and would form the subject matter for his horrific tales for years to come.

During the summer of 1839, a local publisher, Lea & Blanchard, agreed to publish 25 of Poe's stories, all that he had written up to that time. Offering Poe nothing but a few copies for himself, the publisher printed 750 copies of *Tales of the Grotesque and Arabesque*, a 2-volume set of

This illustration from Poe's "Fall of the House of Usher" *represents the line* "But then without those doors there did stand the lofty and enshrouded figure of the Lady Madeline of Usher."

240 pages each. Although according to literary scholars the book contained some of the greatest stories yet written by an American author, it attracted little critical attention and did not even sell out its first printing.

Poe's work at *Burton's* continued at a steady pace, but the more he wrote for the popular journal, the less satisfied he was with his position there. Paid little and resentful of

In 1841, George R. Graham, who bought Burton's, *offered Poe the editorship of the magazine, which he renamed* Graham's Magazine.

Burton's strong editorial hand, Poe resigned his editorship in the spring of 1840. Adding to his discontent was that Burton had decided to sell the magazine and had advertised it for sale in May without first informing his star editor. Of all the reasons for the break, however, the most important was Poe's desire to have a magazine of his own.

Indeed, Poe had never given up the idea of owning and editing his own magazine. As publisher he would no longer be dependent solely on the paltry rates paid to American authors. One of the reasons for the poor compensation to American authors at the time was that no international copyright laws existed. This meant that a publisher could sell works by British or European authors without paying the authors anything and therefore make more money upon the sale of the magazine. If Poe had his own journal, he could choose from among the best of both British and American works and reap the profits himself.

Unfortunately, starting a magazine required capital, and Poe was almost as poor as he had ever been. On June 13, 1840, in an effort to raise both money and support, he announced, in the Philadelphia *Saturday Courier*, the publication of his magazine, called the *Penn*. The prospectus, published in the newspaper, outlined Poe's ideas for the magazine's contents. It would be a journal dedicated to fine literature and to criticism, although he admitted that the years "may have mellowed down the petulance without interfering with the rigor of the critic." The *Penn* would support the "general interests of the republic of letters, without reference to particular regions." Most important, "its aim chiefly shall be to *please*; and this through means of versatility, originality, and pungency." Its cost would be $5 per year, much higher than most other journals of the day, and its first issue would be published in January 1841.

For six months, Poe tried unsuccessfully to raise money for the *Penn*, and on January 1 he was forced to announce a delay in publication for at least three more months. Then, during the winter, he became ill with the flu and was unable to work. With no hope of raising enough capital and in need of money to support his family, Poe agreed, once again, to work on another man's magazine.

Ironically, it was the new owner of *Burton's*, George R. Graham, who offered Poe employment. Graham, already an editor and publisher, had purchased *Burton's* list of 3,500 subscribers, then merged the magazine

One of Aubrey Beardsley's illustrations for "The Murders in the Rue Morgue," the world's first true detective story, depicts the murderer—a gorilla—carrying his victim away. Poe's tale of ratiocination involved solving the crime through the process of rational thought (examination of the crime scene and logical deduction after reviewing the facts).

with his own, called the *Casket*. The resulting journal was called *Graham's Magazine*. Only 27 years old, Graham was an attorney by trade. He hired Poe as the editor of his magazine in April 1841.

Poe's illness during the winter apparently had not prevented him from writing, for he contributed one of his most remarkable stories to the April issue of *Graham's*. "The Murders in the Rue Morgue" was completely different from anything Poe had yet written or, indeed, from anything penned by any author in the history of fiction. Poe called it a "tale of ratiocination," because it involved solving a crime through the process of rational thought and detection.

In the past, other authors, such as the French writer Voltaire and the English philospher and novelist William Godwin (who was also the father of Mary Shelley, the author of *Frankenstein*), had created characters who solved crimes by making wild guesses or by forcing the criminal to confess. Poe, however, created fiction's first true detective in the character of C. Auguste Dupin. Dupin, like the author himself, came from an aristocratic family that disowned him. He spent most of his time reading and had an especially acute analytic mind. In "The Murders in the Rue Morgue," Dupin solved a pair of baffling murders simply by reading newspaper accounts and making a careful examination of the crime scene.

Poe wrote three other tales of ratiocination over the next several years, including "The Mystery of Marie Rogêt," which also had Dupin as the hero, "The Gold-Bug," and "The Purloined Letter." In these tales it is not in the mystery itself that the author seeks to interest the reader, but rather in the successive steps of logic the detective must take to solve it. In this goal, Poe was quite successful.

Sir Arthur Conan Doyle, who in 1877 created Sherlock Holmes, perhaps the most renowned character in detective fiction, later spoke of Edgar Poe's remarkable accomplishment. "Edgar Allen [sic] Poe . . . was the father of the detective tale, and covered its limits so completely that I fail to see how his followers can find any fresh ground which they can confidently call their own."

Poe himself, however, was less enthusiastic about his detective fiction. Several years after "The Murders in the Rue Morgue" was published, he confessed to a fellow author that the tales of ratiocination "owe most of their popularity to being something in a new key. I do not mean that they are not ingenious—but people think them more ingenious than they are—on account of their method and *air* of method." Poe had far greater respect for stories that depended on the creation and sustaining of a mood than those in which clever invention and rational detection held sway.

As Poe continued to expand his repertoire, his standing among his peers slowly rose. He was making more money than he had ever made before—about $1,200 a year— enough for him and his family to move into a comfortable cottage, complete with a garden in the back. After about a year of working for Graham, Poe was able to afford to buy a harp and a piano for his wife, who loved to sing, and furniture for the household. To complete the domestic picture, Virginia and her mother adopted a tortoiseshell kitten, with the apt name of Caterina, to keep them company. Indeed, Poe's home life was as stable and pleasant as it had ever been.

With his creative work proceeding apace and his emotional life so peaceful, Poe had every reason to feel secure. However, despite being a devoted husband, a thoughtful friend, and a prolific writer, Poe was still tempted to drink. Although his problem with alcohol did not seem to interfere with his work, Poe was often seen in a drunken state at one of Philadelphia's many taverns. His reputation as a drunkard would soon outshine his reputation as a writer.

No one can say for certain what compulsion drove Poe to drink. In his story "Eleanora," however, he hinted that the same inner demons also provided him with the inspiration for his stories. "The question is not yet settled," he wrote, "whether madness is or is not the loftiest intelligence—whether much that is glorious, whether all that is profound—does not spring from disease of thought—from moods of mind, exalted at the expense of the general intellect." In fact, his most successful stories revealed a fervid imagination that seemed on the brink of madness, dealing as they did with morbid topics in florid language.

Despite his lapses into drink, Poe continued to further his career. Charles Dickens, the most famous and successful British author of his day, met with Poe during a visit to America in the spring of 1842. No record exists that recounts the meeting, but Dickens must have been impressed with his American colleague, for he brought back to England a copy of *Tales of the Grotesque and Arabesque* in hopes of publishing it there. Although Dickens was unsuccessful, the effort no doubt pleased Poe, who had recently favorably reviewed Dickens's novel *The Old Curiosity Shop*.

Even Henry Wadsworth Longfellow, whom Poe had accused not only of bad writing but also of plagiarism, had apparently been impressed enough with Poe's talent to overlook his insults. In replying to a letter from Poe requesting he submit some work to *Graham's*, Longfellow replied, "All that I have read from your pen has inspired me with a high idea of your power; and I think you are destined to stand among the first romance-writers of the country, if such be your aim."

Another of Poe's acquaintances during his tenure at *Graham's* was Rufus Wilmot Griswold. A handsome young man in his mid-twenties, Griswold was a literary journalist currently preparing an anthology of American poetry. Poe first met him early in 1841, when Griswold agreed to include three of Poe's poems in his collection *The Poets and Poetry of America*. For at least a year the two men apparently shared great respect for one another. In the magazine, Poe described Griswold as someone

The British author Charles Dickens met Poe during a visit to New York in 1842. Dickens greatly admired Poe's writing talent and tried to find a publisher for Tales of the Grotesque and Arabesque *in England.*

whose "knowledge of American literature . . . is not exceeded by that of any man among us." The friendship would not last long, however, for Rufus Griswold was a particularly ambitious and ruthless man.

Throughout 1842, Poe remained remarkably productive. In addition to providing critical reviews and editorial services to *Graham's*, he also wrote and sold several stories, including the terrifying "Masque of the Red Death" and "The Pit and the Pendulum." Nevertheless, he was again growing tired of taking orders from a man he considered his intellectual inferior, and he was equally upset over his low wages.

At the end of two productive years at the helm of *Graham's Magazine*, Poe considered resigning his position. On a visit to the office shortly after informing Graham of his pending decision, Poe was shocked to find none other than Rufus Griswold, his erstwhile friend, occupying his editor's chair. To add insult to injury, Poe discovered that Griswold, a younger man with less experience, was being paid more money than Poe had earned.

From that moment on, Poe and Griswold were locked in an often ugly battle of reputations. Poe denigrated Griswold's work in several reviews, and Griswold spread rumors that exaggerated the frequency and severity of Poe's drinking habits. Although over the years the two occasionally put aside their differences, the end result of their relationship devastated Poe.

With regular work now over for the time being, Poe turned again to his favorite obsession: to own a magazine of his own. Like its unsuccessful predecessor, Poe's new journal would be a high-priced literary publication attracting only the best American poetry, fiction, and criticism, "guiding itself only by the purest rules of art." The only difference between the new magazine and the *Penn* would be the name. In the spring of 1843, Poe began promoting the *Stylus*, a name chosen because the *Penn* seemed to limit the magazine's range to Pennsylvania.

Despite Poe's drinking binges, he continued to be productive in his writing career. In 1842 he wrote the terrifying "Masque of the Red Death" and "The Pit and the Pendulum."

Perhaps because of his steady employment with *Graham's*, Poe was able to attract more support for the *Stylus*. A local illustrator and publisher, Thomas Clarke, offered to become a partner in Poe's venture. It was in Clarke's newspaper, the *Saturday Museum*, that the prospectus for the *Stylus* was first printed. It appeared that Clarke also had some capital to invest if Poe could enlist enough interest, and money, to support a new publication.

One of Poe's important supporters during this period was James Russell Lowell, a poet and essayist from New England. Lowell, only in his mid-twenties himself, had recently attempted to start his own magazine, called the *Pioneer*, which Poe greatly respected and in which one of his most famous stories, "The Tell-Tale Heart," was published. Although poor himself, Lowell vowed to help Poe in any way he could.

As usual, lack of money stood in the way of Poe's dreams. In fact, Poe was so tired of trying to make a living as a writer that he was tempted to find employment in a completely new arena: the U.S. government. A friend, Frederick W. Thomas, had secured for himself a temporary clerkship in the Treasury Department and convinced Poe to seek a similar job in the Philadelphia Customs House. Most government positions paid at least $1,500 a year—a fortune in Poe's eyes—and, according to Thomas, the job would leave plenty of free time in which Poe could write.

After borrowing money from his partner, Clarke, Poe headed for Washington, D.C., to make a personal plea for a job to President John Tyler through his son, Robert Tyler, who was a friend of Thomas's. The trip, however, was a disaster. Thomas was ill and left Poe in the care of a friend, Jesse Dow, who was known to have a fondness for liquor. Dow, perhaps unaware of Poe's problem with alcohol, brought the author to a rowdy Washington party. Nervous and anxious to please his host, Poe drank with the other guests. When Dow later brought Poe to the White House, Robert Tyler felt the author was too intoxicated to meet the president. For four more days, until he was sent home in disgrace, Poe drank and misbehaved, poking fun at government officials at parties and embarrassing his hosts.

Clarke, who was shocked and upset when he learned of Poe's behavior, withdrew his support for the *Stylus*, ending once again Poe's dream of owning a magazine.

Perhaps the most devastating blow to Poe, however, was that his wife, Virginia, was desperately ill, apparently with tuberculosis, the same illness that had taken his mother from him some 21 years before. In June 1842, while singing, Virginia began coughing up blood, a sure sign that the disease had progressed to a lethal stage. Since that time, her health had been failing rapidly.

The thought of losing his wife sent Poe into the depths of despair. After his return to Philadelphia from Washington, Poe's drinking continued. He disappeared for several days, then was brought home, pale and in a state of collapse. Although known to exaggerate, Rufus Griswold later wrote an accurate account (confirmed by others who knew Poe then) of the poet during this period in 1843 and 1844:

> He walked the streets, in madness or melancholy, with lips moving in indistinct curses, or with eyes upturned in passionate prayers . . . and at night, with drenched garments and arms wildly beating the wind and rain, he would speak as if to spirits.

As 1843 drew to an end, Poe managed, between his bouts of drinking, to write new stories, some of which he sold to *Graham's* and other journals. Unfortunately, he soon exhausted his resources in Philadelphia, as he had in Baltimore and Richmond, because of his drinking and his biting comments about his colleagues.

Finally, in April 1844, after almost six years of nearly uninterrupted productivity, Poe decided to leave Philadelphia and move to New York. Taking Virginia with him but leaving Maria Clemm behind to pack up the small household, he returned to New York to make a new start.

An illustration of "The Raven," a poem that first appeared in the New York Evening Mirror *on January 29, 1845. "The Raven" firmly established Poe's renown as a poet.*

7

"The Raven" and Nevermore

JUST ONE WEEK AFTER POE ARRIVED in New York City in April 1844, these headlines blared across the front page of the *New York Sun*: ASTOUNDING NEWS! BY EXPRESS VIA NORFOLK THE ATLANTIC CROSSED IN THREE DAYS! SIGNAL TRIUMPH OF MR. MONCK MASON'S FLYING MACHINE! The story recounted in remarkably realistic detail an incredible journey across the Atlantic made by two gentlemen in a hot-air balloon. The paper sold out two editions, with thousands of customers anxious to read the fantastic tale.

Although the article was unsigned, it bore the unmistakable imprint of Edgar Allan Poe, who later admitted to foisting the story—with the cooperation of the *Sun*'s editors—upon an unsuspecting public. He had created a similar stir nine years earlier when the *Messenger* published "Hans Phaall: A Tale," a story about a balloon trip to the moon. By applying a journalistic tone to an absurd set of facts, he succeeded in fooling some of his readers and at least amusing the rest.

The small New York farm-house that Poe found for himself, his wife, and his mother-in-law was located on what is today 84th Street between Columbus and Amsterdam avenues.

That Poe chose to make such a colorful entrance onto the New York literary stage after his retreat from Philadelphia shows how resilient and optimistic he was, both as a writer and as a man.

Indeed, Poe was eager to take on new challenges. After "The Balloon Hoax" was published, Poe was hired by a small Pennsylvania magazine called the *Columbia Spy* to write a weekly column called "Doings of Gotham." Different from anything he had produced so far, these short articles about New York City gave the author's impressions of the city's architecture, people, and events of the day, providing an invaluable portrait of New York in 1844. Poe contributed just a few of these charming pieces before the magazine ceased publication.

It was during one of his long walks through New York in search of material that Poe found a home for himself, Virginia, and the newly arrived Maria Clemm. A small farmhouse, located on what is today 84th Street between Columbus and Amsterdam avenues, seemed a perfect setting for the family. Set in a peaceful, rural area suitable for Virginia's precarious health, the house was just a short carriage ride to the center of town.

Unfortunately, after the reverberations from "The Balloon Hoax" dissipated, Poe felt that New York was no more welcoming than he had found it to be seven years before. Unable to find work, he decided, for the first time in his professional career, to withdraw from employment in the literary world. While Poe wrote in his study or wandered in the nearby woods, Maria Clemm acted as his agent.

It was Clemm who brought his stories around to the editors at the various journals and she who negotiated the paltry sums he was paid for them. Poe biographer Julian Symons postulates that Poe was paid even less than many of his contemporaries simply because his desperate need for money was so well known.

It was true that Poe seemed particularly inept at day-to-day living. In July 1844 his old friend James Russell Lowell asked Poe to write a small autobiographical sketch for use in a larger piece Lowell was composing for *Graham's*. In it, Poe admitted that he was unable to manage well in the "real" world:

> I have been too deeply conscious of the mutability and evanescence of temporal things, to give any continuous effort to anything—to be consistent in anything. . . . My life has been whim—impulse—passion—a longing for solitude—a scorn of all things present, in an earnest desire for the future.

During the summer of 1844, Poe, deeply worried about Virginia's failing health, wrote a number of strange stories about hypnotism and death. One of them, "Mesmeric Revelation," concerned a man who dies while in a hypnotic trance and reveals the nature of God and heaven and the cruelty of life on earth:

In 1844, James Russell Lowell, an old friend of Poe's, asked Poe to write an autobiographical sketch for inclusion in Graham's. *In the piece, Poe admitted that he was unable to manage well in the "real" world.*

> All things are either good or bad by comparison. . . . *Positive* pleasure is a mere idea. To be happy at any one point we must have suffered at the same. Never to suffer would have been never to have been blessed. . . . The pain of primitive life of Earth, is the sole basis of the bliss of the ultimate life in Heaven.

Poe, who had seen his wife suffer through poverty and now a debilitating, painful illness, must have taken some comfort in the ideas he expressed in this story.

Although Poe managed with Maria Clemm's help to sell a few other stories, including "The Oblong Box" and "The Premature Burial," the family was edging toward starvation. Because Poe seemed reticent, Clemm took it upon herself to find her son-in-law a job. In September, she called upon N. P. Willis, the editor of the *New York Evening Mirror*, who more than once had been the object of Poe's biting criticism. Fortunately, Willis was

An illustration from the story "Mesmeric Revelation" represents the line "A few passes threw Mr. Vankirk into the mesmeric sleep." The story involves a man who dies while in a hypnotic trance and then relates the nature of God and heaven.

impressed both with Poe's talent and with Maria Clemm, whom he later described as "beautiful and saintly with an evidently complete giving up of her life to privation and sorro͙ ͙l tenderness." Willis agreed to hire Poe as a critic ͙ditor at a small salary.

With Maria Clemm's gentle push, Poe reentered the world of letters with typical energy. He moved the family from the farmhouse into a small boardinghouse in the center of town and, as usual, performed his job with both vigor and controversy. In one of his first reviews for the *Mirror*, he once again accused the renowned Longfellow of plagiarism, this time claiming that the writer had stolen material for his play *The Spanish Student* from Poe himself.

This was the opening salvo in an intense literary war waged by Poe against his old enemies, the New England elite. It seemed as if time had only deepened Poe's resentment. In the months and years to come, his battle against the establishment would become ever more bitter and self-destructive.

In January 1845, however, the publication of Poe's poem "The Raven" deflected all attention away from his criticism. Introducing the poem, Willis himself claimed it to be "unsurpassed in English poetry for subtle conception, masterly ingenuity of versification, and consistent sustaining of imaginative life. . . . It will stick to the memory of everybody who reads it."

To compose this remarkable poem, Poe plotted each stanza as if he were plotting a story. While a bereaved lover sits mournfully in his room, grieving over his lost love, Lenore, he hears a tapping. When he opens the door, no one is there. He hears the tapping again and opens the window. In struts a shiny, black-feathered raven that flies up to sit upon the transom ledge. The raven croaks one startling word: *Nevermore.*

> "Prophet!" said I, "thing of evil!—prophet still, if bird
>   or devil!
> By that heaven that bends above us—by that God we both
>   adore—
> Tell this soul with sorrow laden if, within the distant
>   Aidenn,
> It shall clasp a sainted maiden whom the angels name
>   Lenore—
> Clasp a rare and radiant maiden whom the angels name
>   Lenore."
>   Quoth the Raven, "Nevermore!"

The publication of "The Raven" turned Poe into a minor celebrity almost overnight. Widely copied and parodied in

"The Oblong Box" was one of Poe's stories that Maria Clemm tried to sell to help buy food for the family. This illustration from the story depicts the line "In another instant both body and box were in the sea."

journals and newspapers across the country, the poem became a popular favorite as well as a critical success. Poe himself enjoyed a respect he had never known: The publishing company of Wiley & Putnam offered to publish two new volumes of his work. *Tales* by Edgar A. Poe included 12 stories and was released in July; *The Raven and Other Poems* was published later in the year. For the first time in his career Poe was offered a royalty of eight cents a copy on every book that sold.

Even old enemies were willing to applaud Poe's success. Although he continued to lie about Poe's character to anyone who would listen, Rufus Griswold wrote to the poet that spring, requesting material for a new anthology. Poe replied with warmth: "Your letter occasioned me first pain and then pleasure:—pain, because it gave me to see that I had lost, through my own folly, an honorable friend:—pleasure, because I saw in it a hope of reconciliation."

Best of all, Poe seemed on the verge of fulfilling his dream of owning his own magazine. In the spring of 1845, on the recommendation of his friend James Lowell, Poe was offered the editorship of a new publication, the *Broadway Journal*. If Poe agreed to be editor, the two owners of the magazine, Charles F. Briggs and Joseph Bisco, would share with him one-third of the profits.

Unfortunately, Poe managed to alienate Charles Briggs almost immediately—for the same reason he had upset the owners of every magazine he had ever been associated with: his harsh criticisms of fellow authors. Against Briggs's advice, Poe carried over and intensified his feud with Longfellow. For every accusation hurled by Poe, another was sent back with equal fury by the Longfellow camp. In the March 8 issue of the *Weekly Mirror*, Longfellow claimed Poe had stolen "The Raven" from an obscure poem called "The Bird of the Dream," a charge as foolish as any Poe had levied.

In addition to waging the Little Longfellow War, Poe once again let loose his Imp of the Perverse and was found

N. P. Willis, the editor of the Mirror, *was moved by Poe's writing and by Maria Clemm's dedication to the author and agreed to hire Poe as a critic and editor at a small salary.*

on several occasions wandering drunk through the streets of New York. Within just a few months, Briggs took Poe's name off the magazine's masthead, and had Briggs not decided to give over the ownership to his partner, Bisco, it is likely Poe would have been fired.

Instead, it appeared Poe had earned a reprieve. Bisco made a separate agreement with him—Poe would be the sole editor of the *Journal* and split the profits with Bisco. Poe continued to write several critical pieces every week as well as to reprint many of his own poems and stories. In addition, he sold stories to other publications, including *Godey's*, *Graham's*, and the *American Review*. He worked as hard as he ever had before, writing to his friend Thomas, "For the last three or four months I have been working 14 or 15 hours a day. . . . I never knew what it was to be a slave before."

In October 1845, Poe was invited to lecture before James Lowell's Boston literary society. For the first time in more than 15 years, Poe visited the city of his birth and, unfortunately, found it as cold as he ever had. His audience was, after all, well acquainted with his criticisms of their favorite son, Henry Wadsworth Longfellow.

Furthermore, Poe, perhaps under the influence of alcohol, decided not to read "The Raven" but instead substituted one of his earliest and most obscure poems, "Al Aaraaf." Poe was insulted when most of his audience left before he completed the lecture and reading; in the next issue of the *Journal* he wrote of Boston, "Their hotels are bad. Their pumpkin pies are delicious. Their poetry is not so good."

Back in New York he continued to ride the now receding crest of "Raven" fame. Among his most devoted fans were several women poets who both admired Poe's writing and were attracted by his dark, hypnotic charm. He met some of these women at literary parties, including many that took place at the home of Anne Charlotte Lynch at 116 Waverly Place. Other women, such as Frances ("Franny")

This engraving of 35-year-old Poe appeared in Graham's *in February 1845, one month after the publication of "The Raven."*

Sargent Osgood, he first knew through their poetry and only later met them in person; Poe had published a few of Osgood's poems several years before in *Burton's*.

In desperate straits over Virginia's worsening health, Poe began several passionate, if nonsexual, flirtations with his women colleagues. During the spring and summer of 1845, for instance, he and Fanny Osgood exchanged love letters and poems; some of the verses Poe published in the *Journal*. Meanwhile, another poetess, Elizabeth Ellet, also sought Poe's affections in the same way. As innocent as these flirtations may have been, they provided grist for the

"'Be that word our sign of parting, bird or fiend!' I shrieked, upstarting." A line from "The Raven," which was illustrated with this picture in a 1908 edition of Poe's works.

ever-churning rumor mill fed by Poe's professional enemies.

Along with juggling an increasingly complicated personal life, Poe was struggling to make a go of his rapidly foundering magazine. Ironically, no matter how hard he worked, he could not create for the *Journal* the same success he had brought to the *Messenger* or to *Graham's*. After raising money from several longtime supporters, including Bostonian James Lowell and John Kennedy from Baltimore, Poe was forced to close the magazine in January 1846.

His reviews had, however, already set a literary war in motion. Just as he closed up his office, the *Knickerbocker* magazine, edited by Lewis Gaylord Clark, struck a vicious blow, denouncing Poe's character by insisting that "no person connected with the press in this country is entitled to less mercy or consideration." For the next several months the war of the literati raged. Poe even took one of his denouncers, Thomas Dunn English, to court, charging him with libel. Although Poe eventually won the suit and was awarded $492, the damage to his reputation was irreparable.

His family life was equally distressing. Word of his literary "affairs" had evidently reached Virginia, who pleaded with her husband to take her away from the rancor of the city to a rural paradise like the one they had shared two years before. Ever anxious to please his increasingly sickly wife, Poe moved the family to a small farmhouse in Fordham, about 13 miles north of the city, during the spring of 1846. It was in this quaint home that Virginia would spend the last year of her life.

While Maria Clemm nursed her daughter, Poe, increasingly ill himself, worked diligently on a new series of articles. Published in *Godey's Lady's Book*, Poe's "Literati of New York" consisted of 38 biographical and critical sketches about the most famous literary personalities in New York. Unlike most of his past critical essays that have

In October 1845, James Lowell invited Poe to lecture before a Boston literary society. Instead of reading from the immensely popular "The Raven," Poe read one of his earliest and most obscure poems, "Al Aaraaf," upon which this illustration is based.

some basis in literary theory, these pieces contain little more than cruel gossip and biting satire. Indeed, their publication essentially ended Poe's career as a critic.

By the end of 1846, Poe's life was a shambles. A paragraph in the December 15 issue of the *New York Express* announced that "Edgar A. Poe and his wife are both dangerously ill with the consumption . . . they are so far reduced as to be barely able to obtain the necessaries of life." A visitor to the Poe home described the sad scene that winter:

Poe's cottage in Fordham, New York.

[Virginia] lay on the straw bed, wrapped in her husband's greatcoat, with a large tortoiseshell cat on her bosom. The

wonderful cat seemed conscious of her great usefulness. The coat and the cat were the sufferer's only means of warmth, except as her husband held her hands and her mother her feet.

Virginia's long struggle ended. She died on January 29, 1847, at the age of 24, the very same age Poe's mother had also succumbed. A few days later, Virginia was buried in a mausoleum in Fordham belonging to the Poes' landlords. N. P. Willis, Poe's former editor at the *New York Evening Mirror*, attended the ceremony, along with several of Poe's women friends, including Mrs. Louise Shew, who had for more than a year helped Maria Clemm care for her dying daughter. Despite their support, Poe was inconsolable.

The parlor of the cottage. The Poes' new home, located about 13 miles north of New York City, became a rural paradise for Virginia, who was ill with tuberculosis and had heard rumors about Poe's flirtations with his female colleagues.

Poe was inconsolable after the death of Virginia. In the spring of 1847 he wrote "Ulalume," a poem recalling a lover's visits to his beloved's grave.

8

The Death and Afterlife of Poe

THE WINTER AND SPRING OF 1847-48 found Edgar Allan Poe in the throes of grief and illness. From what ailment he suffered remains unknown. His friend Louise Shew, who was the daughter of a physician and had some training in medicine herself, diagnosed Poe with a brain lesion. This, she claimed, would explain his susceptibility to alcohol and his frequent lapses into depression. Whether her diagnosis had any basis in fact, however, is unsubstantiated.

By the spring, after being nursed by Maria Clemm and Louise Shew through fever and grief, Poe once again felt ready to work. In many ways, Virginia's death had released him from the dread her illness bred in him. As he began to work again, he wrote to a friend that spring, "This I can & do endure as becomes a man—it was the horrible oscillation between hope & despair which I could *not* longer have endured without the total loss of reason."

His first composition after Virginia's death was the poem "Ulalume." Although largely considered rambling and unstructured, this verse, recalling a lover's bereaved visits to his lover's grave, was clearly a reflection of the poet's own state of mind.

During the spring, Poe launched into his most ambitious and wide-ranging project yet: the essay "Eureka." Unlike "Theory of Composition" and "The Rationale of Verse," composed the year before, "Eureka" did not deal with the subject of literature or poetry. Instead, this 100-page philosophical and scientific treatise was nothing less than Poe's attempt to sum up his theories about the origin, character, and future of the universe. Its subject matter ran

On January 27, 1847, Poe wrote this letter to Louise Shew, the woman who had nursed Virginia before her death. After the death of his wife, Poe relied on Shew for emotional support.

from the existence of God to the physical properties of electricity and light to an explanation of the law of gravity.

Unfortunately, most critics found the piece to be almost incomprehensible. When Poe did manage to find a publisher, George Putnam, he was paid just $14 for his efforts. In fact, the payment was a mere advance; Putnam forced Poe to sign a document promising to repay the money if the book did not sell. Although Poe apparently was able to keep the money, no more than a few hundred copies of "Eureka" were ever purchased.

The failure of what he called his "prose poem" was made all too clear in February 1848, when Poe delivered a lecture to a literary society in the library of the New York Historical Society. Recalling the reaction to "The Raven" just a few years before, Poe counted on an audience of at least 300. Only 60 people attended. The publication of "Eureka" effectively ended Poe's professional literary career.

For the next year and a half, until his death, Poe was obsessed with the same two goals that had possessed him throughout his life: to own and edit his own magazine and to create a home and a family with a woman devoted to him as a wife.

He turned his attention first to reviving plans for the *Stylus*. Knowing that he had few supporters left in New York, he borrowed money from friends to return to Richmond, Virginia, his hometown and the site of his first success, as editor at the *Messenger*. His homecoming, however, proved too much for his already broken spirit. He stayed there just three weeks in October, until John R. Thompson, the editor of the *Messenger*, put him on a train back to New York, claiming to a friend that Poe had been "horribly drunk and discoursing *Eureka* every night to the audiences of Bar Rooms." He apparently made little or no attempt to obtain subscribers for his own magazine.

In terms of his second goal, that of finding a woman to care for him, Poe was faced with many choices. Louise

"The Bells," a melodic poem that Poe wrote in 1848, was described by a critic as "one of the most successful verbal imitations of sound in the English language."

> The Bells.
>
> By Edgar A. Poe.
>
> I.
>
> Hear the sledges with the bells ——
> Silver bells!
> What a world of merriment their melody foretells
> How they tinkle, tinkle, tinkle,
> In the icy air of night!
> While the stars that oversprinkle
> All the Heavens, seem to twinkle
> With a crystalline delight;
> Keeping time, time, time,
> In a sort of Runic rhyme,

Shew remained a good friend in the months following Virginia's death. It was in her company, and with her help, that he composed one of his most melodic poems, "The Bells," which a critic called "one of the most successful verbal imitations of sound in the English language." Simply by reading a few lines of verse, a reader hears an unmistakable ringing:

> Hear the sledges with the bells— Silver bells!
> *What* a world of merriment their melody foretells!
> How they tinkle, tinkle, tinkle
> In the icy air of night!

But Louise Shew, wary of Poe's increasingly erratic behavior, broke off their relationship at the end of October 1848. Indeed, Poe seemed quite desperate for love and comfort. Two poets, Jane Locke and Estelle Lewis, both sought the poet's attention and, on occasion, helped him financially. For a short time, he appeared to return their affections. But for most of the last year of his life, his heart was torn between two women, Nancy Richmond of Lowell, Massachusetts, whom he called Annie, and Sarah Helen Whitman of Providence, Rhode Island, whom he called Helen.

Poe first became acquainted with Helen Whitman, a poetess of some note, at one of the literary parties held at Anne Charlotte Lynch's sometime during 1847. Helen was evidently quite taken with Poe and composed for him a romantic Valentine verse that she read to the literary group in his absence. He returned the honor, composing a second "To Helen," a 66-line free-verse poem of much less value and character than the first poem, which he wrote in 1824, when he was just 15 years old.

And so their romance began. On the surface, Helen Whitman seemed an unlikely choice for Poe. Nearly 50 years old when she first met Poe, she was not known for her physical beauty, nor was she by any means a great poet. Moreover, she hailed from the heart of New England, Poe's enemy territory. Fairly wealthy, she lived with her sister and mother, both of whom would soon object to her relationship with Edgar Allan Poe.

The poet Sarah Helen Whitman, called Helen, was quite taken with Poe, and he with her. Poe composed a poem in her honor and soon became romantically involved with her.

In contrast to Helen Whitman was Annie Richmond, a petite, pretty woman six years younger than Poe. He met her in July 1848, when he lectured in Lowell to raise money for his trip south. Happily married to a successful paper manufacturer, Annie was described by Poe as "the perfection of natural, in contradistinction from artificial, *grace*."

To both Helen and Annie, Poe seemed equally attached. He wrote to Helen about their first meeting:

> As you entered the room . . . I felt, for the first time in my life, and tremblingly acknowledged, the existence of spiritual influences altogether out of the reach of reason. I saw that you were *Helen—my* Helen—the Helen of a thousand dreams.

And to Annie only a few weeks later he wrote:

> . . . so long as I think you comprehend in some measure the fervor with which I adore you, *so* long, no worldly trouble can ever render me absolutely wretched. But oh, *my darling, my* Annie, my own sweet *sister* Annie, my *pure* beautiful angel—*wife* of my soul—to be mine hereafter & *forever in the Heavens*.

Rosalie, Poe's sister, was a poor, retarded woman of 36 when Poe visited her in Richmond in 1849.

That Poe could harbor such passion for two women at the same time is unlikely. Instead, it appears that Poe was on the edge of insanity and deep despair, crying out for comfort in the only way he knew how—the written word.

Poe spent the next several months scurrying back and forth between Lowell, Providence, and New York. At one point, it seemed certain that he would marry Helen Whitman; then her mother broke off the engagement. They reconciled for a time; then Poe himself called the marriage off, feeling in his heart that Annie was his own true love.

In the midst of these melodramatic emotional events, Poe was contacted by a young man of 21 named Edward Patterson. Patterson lived in Oquawka, Illinois, had just inherited his father's newspaper, and was anxious to publish a magazine as well. He wrote that he wanted the contents of the magazine to be under Poe's exclusive control and that he would provide the funding if Poe could obtain a subscription list of 1,000 subscribers. Once again, it seemed that his beloved *Stylus* was within reach.

Poe headed for Richmond, where he believed the most support for the journal could be found. Before he left, however, he seemed to Maria Clemm particularly morose and melancholy. On leaving, Poe told her that he doubted he would ever see her again. Nevertheless, his parting words to her, as she later recalled, were "God bless you, my own darling mother. Do not fear for Eddy! See how good I will be while I am away from you, and will come back to love and comfort you."

Word came to her 10 days later that Poe had taken ill in Philadelphia, where he had stopped to visit old friends. According to John Sartain, an engraver who saw Poe during this period, the poet was delirious, perhaps from drink or fever, during his short stay there.

By the time he reached Richmond on July 14, 1849, he was in better spirits. While staying at the Swan Tavern, he visited with old friends, gave a few lectures to raise money, and saw his younger sister, Rosalie, now a poor, retarded woman of 36. As for the *Stylus*, Poe seemed to put his plans for developing the magazine on hold, perhaps, as biographer Julian Symons postulates, aware that he was physically and intellectually incapable of such a task.

Instead, once again, Poe turned his attention to matters of the heart. One of the many old friends to greet him was Sarah Elmira Shelton, his first true love. Now a wealthy widow, Shelton rekindled her decades-old romance with Poe, and plans were made for the two to be married. In September, Poe wrote to Maria of the engagement but let it slip that he still adored Annie Richmond. It appeared that Poe was merely after Shelton's money.

Poe remained in Richmond for almost three months before deciding to return to New York to wrap up his

Sarah Elmira Shelton, Poe's first true love, was a wealthy widow when Poe met her again in Richmond in 1849. Poe was emotionally desperate at this time; after rekindling his romance with Shelton, Poe wrote to Maria Clemm that he still loved Annie Richmond.

affairs there. On his way home he planned to stop in Baltimore and Philadelphia to conduct business. He left the city on a boat bound for Baltimore on September 27.

What happened during the next several days is unknown. On October 3, Dr. J. E. Snodgrass, one of Poe's former editors, was given a note explaining the fate of Edgar Allan Poe. According to a 1991 biography by Kenneth Silverman, Poe was found unconscious and poorly clad in a Baltimore tavern. Snodgrass rushed to the aid of his old friend, taking him by carriage to Washington College Hospital. Poe died, of drink or of some unknown ailment, on October 7, 1849. He was 40 years old.

His last coherent words, as recalled by the attending physician, Dr. Moran, were "It's all over now; write 'Eddy is no more.'" Poe was buried on October 8, 1849, in the cemetery of Westminster Presbyterian Church near the corner of Fayette and Green streets, in Baltimore. In attendance were just eight or nine people, including Neilson Poe, the author's cousin; a former classmate from the University of Virginia; and a relative of Maria Clemm's, the Reverend W. T. D. Clemm. Maria Clemm herself did not learn of her son-in-law's death until after his burial.

After Poe's death, his reputation as a writer and a man was tarnished by none other than his old enemy, Rufus W. Griswold. Maria Clemm, under the impression that her son-in-law desired Griswold to be his literary executor, signed over to him a complete power of attorney. Into the hands of his enemy, then, went Edgar Allan Poe's life's work.

Two years later, Griswold published the first edition of Poe's collected works. Its foreword was a biographical sketch, cunningly created by Griswold to paint the poet in the worst possible light. By innuendo, half-truths, and lies, Griswold showed Poe to be a drunkard, an opium addict, and a selfish ne'er-do-well who did nothing but borrow money and slander the good names of all he knew. Although several of Poe's contemporaries rallied to Poe's defense, Griswold's account was the only major biographical material published for many years. His lies were accepted as truth for several decades.

Since then, however, a more objective view of this troubled genius has emerged. All over the world, his gifts as a poet, a storyteller, and a critic have been admired. One of his greatest champions was the 19th-century French poet Charles Baudelaire, who first translated many of Poe's works. Paul Valéry, a French poet of the 20th century, claimed, "Poe is the only impeccable writer. He was never mistaken." Russian writer Fyodor Dostoyevski admired Poe as well, summing up quite succinctly his troubled, complicated life. "What a strange, though enormously talented writer," he wrote, "that Edgar Poe!"

Perhaps more than a poet, storyteller, or even a critic, Poe should be remembered as a visionary and a dreamer. His keen analytic mind and fervid imagination brought the netherworld of nightmares and fantasies alive on the page. Poe himself described his greatest gift in his short story "Mesmeric Revelation":

> They who dream by day are cognizant of many things which escape the dreamers by night. In their grey visions, they obtain glimpses of eternity, and thrill, in awaking, to find that they have been on the verge of the great secret. In snatches, they learn something of the wisdom which is of good, and more of that mere knowledge which is of evil.

Poe was buried in the cemetery of Westminster Presbyterian Church in Baltimore, Maryland, on October 8, 1849.

Further Reading

Allen, Hervey. *Israfel: The Life and Times of Edgar Allan Poe*. New York: Durang, 1926.

Benet, Laura. *Young Edgar Allan Poe*. New York: Dodd, Mead, 1941.

Bittner, William Robert. *Poe: A Biography*. Boston: Little, Brown, 1962.

Bloom, Harold, ed. *Edgar Allan Poe*. Modern Critical Views. New York: Chelsea House, 1985.

Campbell, Killis. *Poe in Relation to His Times*. Chapel Hill: University of North Carolina Press, 1923.

Gill, William Fearing. *The Life of Edgar Allan Poe*. New York: Widdleton, 1878.

Haines, Charles. *Edgar Allan Poe: His Writing and Influence*. New York: Watts, 1974.

Haining, Peter, ed. *The Edgar Allan Poe Scrapbook*. New York: Schocken Books, 1978.

Harrison, James Albert. *The Life and Letters of Edgar Allan Poe*. New York: Crowell, 1903.

Hoffman, Daniel. *Poe Poe Poe Poe Poe Poe Poe*. Garden City, NY: Doubleday, 1972.

Hyneman, Esther F. *Edgar Allan Poe: An Annotated Bibliography of Books and Articles*. Boston: Hall, 1974.

Kesterton, David B., ed. *Critics on Poe*. Coral Gables: University of Miami Press, 1973.

Levin, Harry. *The Power of Blackness: Hawthorne, Poe, Melville*. Athens: Ohio University Press, 1989.

Ransome, Arthur. *Edgar Allan Poe: A Critical Study*. Norwood, PA: Norwood Editions, 1978.

Silverman, Kenneth. *Edgar A. Poe: Mournful and Never-ending Remembrance*. New York: HarperCollins, 1991.

Symons, Julian. *The Tell-Tale Heart: The Life and Works of Edgar Allan Poe*. New York: Penguin Books, 1981.

Edgar Allan Poe
The Works

The Best of Poe. West Haven, CT: Academic Industries, 1984.

The Complete Poems of Edgar Allan Poe. Edited by Louise Untermeyer. New York: Heritage Press, 1943.

The Complete Poetry and Selected Criticisms of Edgar Allan Poe. Edited by Allen Tate. New York: New American Library, 1968.

The Complete Stories and Poems of Edgar Allan Poe. Garden City, NY: Doubleday, 1966.

Great Tales and Poems of Edgar Allan Poe. New York: Washington Square Press, 1951.

The Letters of Edgar Allan Poe. Edited by John Ward Ostrom. New York: Gordian Press, 1966.

The Science Fiction of Edgar Allan Poe. Edited by Harold Beaver. New York: Penguin Books, 1976.

The Tales of Poe. Edited by Harold Bloom. New York: Chelsea House, 1987.

The Tell-Tale Heart and Other Works. New York: Bantam Books, 1982.

The Unabridged Edgar Allan Poe. Illustrated by Suzanne Clee. Philadelphia: Running Press, 1983.

Chronology

1809	Born Edgar Poe on January 19 to Elizabeth and David Poe, two actors
1811	Poe's mother dies. Poe taken in by John and Frances Allan, a Virginia couple, but never legally adopted
1815–20	Poe travels with Allans to Scotland and London. Studies at a boarding school in Chelsea and the Manor House School at Stoke Newington
1820–25	Attends private schools in Richmond, Virginia; meets Jane Stanard, to whom he dedicates his poem "To Helen" several years later
1826	Enters University of Virginia in Charlottesville; forced to leave by John Allan because of gambling debts
1827	Publishes first book of poetry, *Tamerlane and Other Poems*; enlists in the U.S. Army
1828–29	Honorably discharged from army after serving at Fort Moultrie, Sullivans Island, South Carolina; Frances Allan dies; Poe visits relatives in Baltimore, including his aunt Maria Clemm and her daughter, Virginia; *Al Aaraaf, Tamerlane, and Minor Poems* is published
1830–31	Enters West Point; later court-martialed; moves to New York, where he publishes *Poems by Edgar A. Poe, Second Edition;* moves to Baltimore to live with the Clemms
1832	Short story "Metzengerstein" is published
1833–34	Poe wins $50 prize for best short story in *Saturday Visitor*; John Allan dies without mentioning Poe in his will
1835	Moves to Richmond to join staff of *Southern Literary Messenger*; fired for drinking on the job; returns to Baltimore; is later rehired; brings Maria Clemm and Virginia with him to Richmond
1836	Officially marries Virginia Clemm, his 14-year-old cousin; has prolific year, publishing numerous reviews, poems, essays, and stories for the *Messenger*; fired once again from the *Messenger* for drinking

1837–38	Moves to New York to write for the *New York Review,* which suspends publication because of nationwide financial crisis; *The Narrative of Arthur Gordon Pym* is published; the Poes move to Philadelphia
1839–40	Poe joins staff of *Burton's Gentleman's Magazine* and publishes "The Fall of the House of Usher," "William Wilson," and "Morella"; *Tales of the Grotesque and Arabesque* is published; Poe resigns from *Burton's* after general disagreements with owner; own plan for starting new magazine, the *Penn,* fails
1841–42	Poe becomes successful editor of *Graham's Magazine* in Philadelphia; creates genre of the mystery story, writing "The Gold-Bug," "The Murders in the Rue Morgue," and "The Mystery of Marie Rogêt"; lapses into drink and is fired once again; attempts to found a new magazine, the *Stylus,* but fails; Virginia becomes ill with tuberculosis
1844	Poe moves to New York; becomes editor of the *New York Evening Mirror*
1845	Publishes "The Raven," *Tales,* and *The Raven and Other Poems*; becomes editor of the *Broadway Journal*
1846	Leaves *Journal* because of bankruptcy; moves to Fordham, New York, with Clemm and Virginia; publishes several articles in *Godey's Lady's Book,* "Literati of New York," a series of biographical sketches of current authors and their work
1847–48	Virginia dies January 29; Poe's own health fails; Poe searches for female companionship with Louise Shew, Sarah Helen Whitman, Nancy "Annie" Richmond, and others; publishes major essay, "Eureka," and several poems, including "For Annie," "Ulalume," "Annabel Lee," and "The Bells"
1849	In a state of depression and drinking steadily; on October 3, Poe is found delirious in Baltimore; dies on October 7

Index

PICTURE CREDITS

Suzanne LeVert is the author of Chelsea House's 14-volume series LET'S DISCOVER CANADA. She is the author of four other books for young readers, including *The Sakharov File*, a biography of Russian physicist Andrey Sakharov, which was selected as a Notable Book by the National Council for the Social Studies. Her other works include *AIDS: In Search of a Killer*, *The Doubleday Book of Famous Americans*, and *New York*. She lives in Cambridge, Massachusetts.

Vito Perrone is Director of Teacher Education and Chair of Teaching, Curriculum, and Learning Environments at Harvard University. He has previous experience as a public school teacher, a university professor of history, education, and peace studies (University of North Dakota), and as dean of the New School and the Center for Teaching and Learning (both at the University of North Dakota). Dr. Perrone has written extensively about such issues as educational equity, humanities curriculum, progressive education, and evaluation. His most recent books are: *A Letter to Teachers: Reflections on Schooling and the Art of Teaching*; *Enlarging Student Assessment in Schools*; *Working Papers: Reflections on Teachers, Schools, and Communities*; *Visions of Peace*; and *Johanna Knudsen Miller: A Pioneer Teacher*.